Nikolai Duffy

Relative Strangeness
Reading Rosmarie Waldrop

Shearsman Books

Published in the United Kingdom in 2013 by
Shearsman Books Ltd
50 Westons Hill Drive
Emersons Green
BRISTOL
BS16 7DF

Shearsman Books Ltd Registered Office
30–31 St. James Place, Mangotsfield, Bristol BS16 9JB
(this address not for correspondence)

ISBN 978-1-84861-277-8
First Edition

Copyright © Nikolai Duffy, 2013.

The right of Nikolai Duffy to be identified as the author of this work has been asserted by him in accordance with the Copyrights, Designs and Patents Act of 1988.
All rights reserved.

Contents

Preface

Between Luggage and Language	9
Blindsights	13
Curvature	17

Relative Strangeness

All Words Are Ajar	23
'To Peel Off Childhood Like So Many Skins'	31
Music Was Everywhere	36
'Since I Cannot Put the World to Rights, I Speak of Love'	42
Burning Deck	47
Bottom Line Abacus	55
Exploring and Maintaining	66
Collage	71
Between, Always	78
Stutter-Flow: *The Road Is Everywhere or Stop This Body*	83
Linearity in Pieces: *Nothing Has Changed*	89
Prose Poems	93
Short Circuits	97
Another Language	110
Theories of Translation	116
All Strange Away: Translating Jabès	127
Shall We Escape Analogy	131
The Caesura	139
Poetry and Politics	146
Disaster	155
'Something Else Than a Stretch of Earth': Living in America	161
Bluff	169
Bibliography	172
Acknowledgements	182
About the Author	183

'Think of the power. Of a single word. Like for example "fact." When I know what matters. Is between.'
—Rosmarie Waldrop, *Blindsight*

'One thinks that one is tracing the outline of the thing's nature over and over again, and one is merely tracing round the frame through which we look at it.'
—Ludwig Wittgenstein, *Philosophical Investigations*

'And it is by glimpses that we come to know anything that has any complexity.'
—Rosmarie Waldrop, 'Between, Always'

Preface

Between Luggage and Language

Even when catching the slow boat from Europe to America, as Rosmarie Waldrop did in 1958, sometimes the rate of travel can be of such a speed that it takes time for the mind to catch up with the body. At the point of crossing is registered the space of between. So it is, suddenly, that the road is already everywhere and it is not always possible to stop a body once it is in motion. Besides, letters written in transit do not, necessarily, always reach their destination, especially when hands are otherwise concerned with holding onto the relative strangeness of luggage and language left behind.

As Gertrude Stein has it, 'nobody knows what the contemporariness is. In other words, they don't know where they are going, but they are on their way.'[1] Or as Waldrop comments in interview:

> what matters is not things but what happens between them. Or if you take the linguistic model, it is not the phoneme but the connection of phonemes that makes language, the differences in the sequence [...] The gaps keep the questions in relation.[2]

'My key words,' Waldrop writes in her essay, 'Alarms and Excursions,' 'would be exploring and maintaining; exploring a forest not for the timber that might be sold, but to understand it as a world and to keep this world alive.'[3]

For Waldrop, poetry is the taking place of language in the spaces between words. Throughout her writing there is the sense that language can be experienced only as fissure, gap, aperture, an 'empty middle' into which the possibility of meaning simultaneously both enters and escapes. As one of the sections in her 1993 work, *Lawn of Excluded Middle*, has it:

> Emptiness is imperative for feeling to take on substance, for its vibrations to grow tangible, a faintly trembling beam that

---

[1] Gertrude Stein, 'How Writing is Written,' *The Previously Uncollected Writings of Gertrude Stein*, Vol. II, ed. Robert Haas (Los Angeles: Black Sparrow Press, 1974) p.29.
[2] Joan Retallack, 'A Conversation with Rosmarie Waldrop,' *Contemporary Literature*, Vol. 40, No. 3 (Autumn, 1999) p.349
[3] Rosmarie Waldrop, 'Alarms and Excursions,' *The Politics of Poetic Form: Poetry and Public Policy*, ed. Charles Bernstein (New York: Roof Books, 1990) p.46.

supports the whole edifice.⁴

'Gaps', 'questions', 'exploring' and 'relation' are central terms in Waldrop's experience of the world, not just of poetry; they are words that resurface repeatedly, carried in each day's clothing. They are also clue to Waldrop's frequent critical reference to Charles Olson's insistence that:

> At root (or stump) what *is*, is no longer THINGS but what happens BETWEEN things, these are the terms of the reality contemporary to us—and the terms of what we are.⁵

No longer one single voice. A multiple meaning. The shadow zone becomes an element of structure. Blanchot's 'other kind of interruption,' which:
> introduces waiting, which measures the distance between two speakers, not the reducible distance, but the irreducible [...] Now what is at stake is the strangeness between us.⁶

Here, as elsewhere, Waldrop's poetry is organised by a spatial imagination: the topography of thinking is the topography of the page.⁷

* * *

A sequence of fragments seems the most appropriate form for a work of this kind, introductory, surveying, essentially personal, marked, as with all things, by my own reading and preoccupations. 'Maybe,' Waldrop writes, 'the essence of the fragment is that it cuts out explanation, an essential act of poetry.'⁸ It constitutes, Waldrop continues, a 'lessening of distinctness, of "identity."'⁹ I do not claim to be comprehensive. Nor do I mean to speak for Waldrop or her work but simply to speak about

---

⁴ Rosmarie Waldrop, *Lawn of Excluded Middle* (Providence, RI: Tender Buttons, 1993) p.14.
⁵ Charles Olson, 'Projective Verse,' *Human Universe and Other Essays*, ed. Donald Allen (New York: Grove, 1967) p.123.
⁶ Rosmarie Waldrop, 'The Ground is the Only Figure,' *Dissonance (if you are interested)* (Tuscaloosa, AL: The University of Alabama Press, 2005) p.227.
⁷ See also 'Christine Hume and Rosmarie Waldrop in Conversation,' *12x12: Conversations in 21ˢᵗ Century Poetry and Poetics*, ed. Christina Mengert and Joshua Marie Wilkinson (Iowa City: University of Iowa Press, 2009) p.254.
⁸ Waldrop, 'The Ground is the Only Figure,' p.227.
⁹ ibid, p.231.

some of its aspects, its various senses of poetics, the shifting relationships between theory and practice, to draw out a number of examples and to trace certain lines of thinking and shifts of approach.

I do not always know where I am in Waldrop's work. My reading, often, is a balance between glimpses and fades, connections and gaps. Semantic fields slide and frames of reference come and go. As Waldrop says of the work of Edmond Jabès which serves equally for a statement about my own reading of Waldrop, 'passages I thought I understood are suddenly incomprehensible again.'[10] 'To continue,' Waldrop goes on to write. 'To carry from one place to another. To continue thinking, to think another place, another perspective. The content of memory changes as I approach it from a different place, myself a different person.'[11] So it is with writing, opinion, thought: everything provisional, of its time, its moment, everything in movement. As Michael Schmidt observes, 'there is something gratuitous and [...] sacramental in what poetry can do. If I understood it, I would leave it behind. Because I don't understand, quite, and my sense of a poem changes as the years change, it stays with me irreducibly.'[12] So much depends upon this 'quite'.

The reasons why are, no doubt, both complex and commonplace. Things change. Life shifts. I have felt, and feel, an affinity to Waldrop's project, for many reasons, not all of which are clear, and most of which are not fully formalised. I feel close to the ways in which Waldrop pieces different texts together, the way she writes, her making. Her rhythms *feel* familiar. Most often, my engagement with Waldrop's writing is no less intuitive than that.

But Waldrop's work also strikes a strange chord inside me, sets off tangential lines of thought, sparks questions which appear at once proximate, naturally occurring, and vertiginous, questions which I don't necessarily recognise as my own but which *feel* familiar; and at different times of the day different aspects feel familiar, different parts elusive. This difference is the site of my reading. And anyway, as Waldrop counsels, it is 'better to trust to the sudden detours, hidden alleys, unexpected corners imagination takes us to' than try to map it out, close it down.[13] Things are not always straightforward.

---

[10] Rosmarie Waldrop, *Lavish Absence: Recalling and Rereading Edmond Jabès* (Middletown, CT: Wesleyan University Press, 2002) p.104.
[11] Waldrop, *Lavish Absence*, p. 149.
[12] Michael Schmidt, 'A Little Carcanet Anthology,' *The North*, No.48 (2011), p.42.
[13] Waldrop, *Lavish Absence*, p.110.

Bobbi Lurie:

I want to write about the humor, sense of playfulness, openness and experimentation in Rosmarie Waldrop's work. I want to write about her signature use of the fragmented 'I' which gives me the sense that I am standing inside the words themselves. It is clear to me as I think of these things that 'what' I 'think' of Rosmarie Waldrop's work is not a 'what' or a 'process of thinking' at all. I am made increasingly aware of how the gaps in Rosmarie Waldrop's descriptions seem to hover over some unnamed edge which forces me to stop thinking for seconds at a time and brings a sense of wholeness in the reading itself. I sit down and try to describe this. At turns I feel I am getting too analytical, then too intellectual, then it seems I am becoming too mystical, too abstract, and then, in the end, too ridiculous.[14]

---

[14] Bobbi Lurie, 'Meditation on Certainty,' *How2*, Vol. 1. No. 8 (Fall 2002), http://www.asu.edu/pipercwcenter/how2journal/archive/online_archive/v1_8_2002/current/readings/lurie.htm, accessed 12 December 2011.

Blindsights

Edmond Jabès has commented how 'we always start out from a written text and come back to the text to be written, from the sea to the sea, from the page to the page.'[1] 'In the beginning is hermeneutics,' repeats Jacques Derrida.[2] There always emerges on the page before us a blank spot, a *blindsight*, that experience where, according to the neuroscientist, Antonio R. Damasio, a person actually sees more than they are consciously aware. It is, strangely, an experience of disassociation, vision without visual consciousness. What counts is how that blindsight is read.

The notion that all writing is, in one form or another, a process of re-writing has a long history, stretching back at least as far as Moses' breaking of the tablets or the Kabbalistic tradition of the breaking of the Vessels, where, according to Luria, God's light proved too much for the vessels meant to contain it and the vessels displaced or shattered. In both cases, the world, here and now, is out of place, composed of the shards of this broken light, these shattered words. As Waldrop notes, according to the Zohar, 'in every word shine multiple lights.'[3]

According to Gershom Scholem, as a result of the Breaking of the Vessels, 'nothing remains in its proper place. Everything is somewhere else.'[4] The breaking, Stanford L. Drob suggests, implies that all concepts, values, systems and beliefs are inadequate containers for the phenomena they are meant to hold and circumscribe. As such, Drob argues, 'the Breaking of the Vessels provides a caution against being satisfied with any of the interpretations or constructions we place upon our experience, texts, and world.'[5]

Susan Handelman:

> Thus in Kabbalah, it is not only the tablets of the law that are broken. The universe itself has undergone a primordial

---

[1] Edmond Jabès, *The Book of Margins*, trans. Rosmarie Waldrop (Chicago and London: The University of Chicago Press, 1993) p.40; quoted in *Lavish Absence*, p.109.
[2] Jacques Derrida, 'Edmond Jabès and the Question of the Book,' *Writing and Difference*, trans. Alan Bass (London: Routledge, 2001) p.81.
[3] Waldrop, *Lavish Absence*, p.20.
[4] Gershom Scholem, *On the Kabbalah and Its Symbolism*, trans. Ralph Manheim (New York: Schocken, 1969) p.112.
[5] Stanford L. Drob, 'Jacques Derrida and the Kabbalah,' *The New Kabbalah* (2006), http://www.newkabbalah.com/JDK.pdf, accessed 12 February 2012.

shattering; God has withdrawn; the Vessels are broken; the divine sparks are lost in the material world. As Scholem reads it, Kabbalah is a great myth of exile.[6]

In reference to Jabès, Maurice Blanchot describes rabbinic exegesis as a double movement of response and distance. 'The dignity and importance of exegesis in the rabbinic tradition,' Blanchot writes, consists of the way in which 'the written law, the unoriginal text of the origin, must always be taken on by the commenting voice—taken on, but unjoined, in this dis-junction that is the measure of its infinity.'[7]

Here reading well involves being out of place, unsure, unsteady; it entails equivocation. It is to set off, to wander, to go looking, but to find myself travelling in circles, further away, elsewhere. In so doing, it necessitates that such reading be counter-intuitive, that it proceed in fits and starts, with questions and effacements, in manners always turning, always bouncing against the limit of what it has not been quite possible to say: blindsights, pieces. The origin is always foreign and the space of commentary an open field.

Rosmarie Waldrop: 'The spark given off by the edges of the shards, the fragments, is stronger the more abrupt the cut, the more strongly it makes us feel the lack of transition, the more disparate the surrounding texts.'[8]

Waldrop, again: 'I love David Mendelson's false etymology that derives the word "mosaic" from Moses, from the breaking of the tablets.'[9]

Influenced by such readings, Edmond Jabès has written how, 'by turning away from the tablets, the chosen people gave Moses a crucial lesson in reading. The destroyed book allows us to read the book.'[10] As Gary Mole glosses:

> for Jabès the breaking of the tablets into an infinite number of fragments initiates fragmentary writing itself, a form of nonformal writing that escapes generic classification by

---

[6] Susan Handelman, *The Sin of the Book*, ed. Eric Gould (Lincoln: University of Nebraska Press, 1985) p.76; quoted in *Lavish Absence*, p.21.
[7] Maurice Blanchot, 'Traces,' *Friendship*, trans. Elizabeth Rottenberg (Stanford, CA: Stanford University Press, 1997) p. 224.
[8] Waldrop, *Lavish Absence*, p.21.
[9] ibid, p.19.
[10] Edmond Jabès, *El, or the Last Book*, trans. Rosmarie Waldrop (Middletown, CT: Wesleyan University Press, 1984) pp.39-40; quoted in *Lavish Absence*, p.19.

undermining the very notions of genre. God's attempt to unify the fragmentary, Jabès would argue, is the significance of the renewal of the tablets in Exodus 34, which Jabès interprets in terms of resemblance [...] The second set of tablets that God is constrained to give to Moses permits the reading of the first set, which only Moses had read, while maintaining the break that is their difference.[11]

Similarly, for Blanchot, 'it is very striking that in a certain tradition of the book [...] what is called the "written Torah" preceded the "oral Torah", the latter subsequently giving rise to a version written down, which alone constitutes the Book.'[12] 'There is an enigmatic proposition to thought in this,' Blanchot continues. 'Nothing precedes writing. Yet the writing of the first tablets becomes legible only after and through their having been broken.'[13] In other words, Blanchot argues, it means there is no 'original word,' or as Waldrop has it, 'the blank page is not blank.'[14] Rather, 'the Tablets of the Law were broken when still only barely touched by the divine hand [...] and were written again, but not in their original form, so that it is from an already destroyed word that man learns the demand that must speak to him: there is no real first understanding, no initial and unbroken word, as if one could never speak except the second time, after having refused to listen and having taken a distance in regard to the origin.'[15] Or as Blanchot writes elsewhere, 'you will never know what you have written, even if you have written only to find this out.'[16]

In his remarkable study of Talmudic reading, *The Burnt Book*, Marc-Alain Ouaknin defines Talmudic thinking as an 'open dialectic.'[17] Talmudic study, Ouaknin explains, is based on a notion of *Mahloket*, or dialogue, that is, a modality of thinking that constantly opens itself to its own contestation. 'The Master of the Talmud', Ouaknin writes,

---

[11] Gary D. Mole, *Levinas, Blanchot, Jabès: Figures of Estrangement* (Gainseville, FL: University Press of Florida, 1997) p.87.
[12] Maurice Blanchot, *L'Entretien Infini* (Paris: Gallimard, 1971) p.630; quoted in Mole, *Levinas*, p.87.
[13] Blanchot, *L'Entretien*, p.631; quoted Mole, p.87.
[14] Rosmarie Waldrop, *Ceci n'est pas Rosmarie* (Providence, RI: Burning Deck, 2002) p.91.
[15] Blanchot, 'Traces,' p.224.
[16] Maurice Blanchot, 'After the Fact,' *Vicious Circles: Two Fictions and After the Fact*, trans. Paul Auster (Barrytown, NY: Station Hill Press, 1985) p.59.
[17] Marc-Alain Ouaknin, *The Burnt Book: Reading the Talmud*, trans. Llewellyn Brown (Princeton, NJ: Princeton University Press, 1995) p. 84.

'[...] seeks to be shaken up, to be disturbed, to suffer setbacks, to be overwhelmed.'[18] Fragile and always on the move, *Mahloket* does not synchronise truth as in, for example, Platonic dialogue, but is, rather, diachronic. *Mahloket* seeks to set its 'reading' to an interminable questioning; it takes place in the 'interrelational space' between itself and the enigma (the text) it seeks to engage.[19] In Waldrop's phrase, it is to be found 'in the margins that let the words breathe.'[20] Edmond Jabès develops this sense of dialogue when, in *The Book of Dialogue*, he writes:

> There is *pre-dialogue*, our slow or feverish preparation for dialogue. Without any idea of how it will proceed, which form it will take, without being able to explain it, we are convinced in advance that the dialogue has already begun: a silent dialogue with an absent partner.
>
> Then afterwards, there is *post-dialogue* or after-silence. For what we managed to say to the other in our exchange of words—says virtually nothing but this silence, silence on which we are thrown back by any unfathomable, self-centred word whose depth we vainly try to sound.
>
> Then finally, there is what could have been the actual dialogue, vital, irreplaceable, but which, alas, does not take place: it begins the very moment we take leave of one another and return to our solitudes.[21]

This inter-relational space, this between point, is everything. It is the ground of thinking, writing, reading, discussing; a zone of movement, of crossings and of crossings out. Indeed, as Ouaknin notes, *Mahloket* 'is possible because the law is *Halakhah*: the etymological meaning of this term being "walking," "step."'[22]

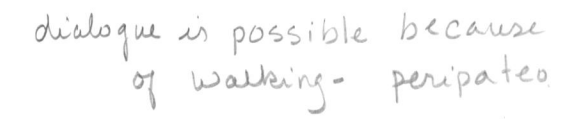

---

[18] Ouaknin, *The Burnt Book*, p. 86.
[19] ibid, pp. 84 and 87.
[20] Waldrop, 'Silence, the Devil, and Jabès,' *Dissonance*, p.148.
[21] Edmond Jabès, *The Book of Dialogue*, trans. Rosmarie Waldrop (Middletown, CT: Wesleyan University Press, 1987) p.7.
[22] Ouaknin, *op. cit*, p. 19.

Curvature

Maurice Blanchot has referred to the relation between text and commentary as having the form of 'curvature,' such that 'the relations of A to B will never be direct, symmetrical, or reversible [...] One can see which solutions will prove inappropriate to such a problem: a language of assertion and answer, for example, or a linear language of simple development, that is to say, *a language where language itself would not be at stake.*'[1]

In his 'In Place of a Foreword' Edmond Jabès writes that '[a] good reader is, first of all, a sensitive, curious, demanding reader. In reading, he follows his intuition.'[2] Jabès goes on to explain that intuition would involve, for example, entering a text not directly but roundabout; and even then, Jabès cautions, when one has wandered, taken many paths, 'at no moment has one left one's own.'[3]

The American scholar Gerald Bruns writes of the way in which 'poetry *exposes* thinking to language, to its strangeness or otherness, its refusal to be contained within categories and propositions, its irreducibility to sameness and identity, its resistance to sense—in short, its denial of our efforts to speak it [...] poetry is the letting-go of language.'[4]

In his *Problems of Dostoyevsky's Poetics*, Mikhail Bakhtin comments the following: 'Imagine a dialogue of two persons in which the statements of the second speaker are omitted [...] The second speaker is present invisibly, his words are not there, but deep traces left by these words have a determining influence on all the present and visible words of the first speaker. We sense that this is a conversation, although only one person is speaking, and it is a conversation of the most intense kind, for each present, uttered word responds to and reacts with its every fiber to the invisible speaker, points to something outside itself, beyond its own limits, to the unspoken words of another person.'[5]

---

[1] Maurice Blanchot, *The Infinite Conversation*, trans. Susan Hanson (Minneapolis and London: University of Minnesota Press, 1993) p.6.
[2] Edmond Jabès, 'In Place of a Foreword' in *From the Book to the Book: An Edmond Jabès Reader*, trans. Rosmarie Waldrop (Hanover and London: Wesleyan University Press, 1991) p.5.
[3] Jabès, *op. cit.*, p.5.
[4] Gerald L. Bruns, *Heidegger's Estrangements: Language, Truth and Poetry* (New Haven: Yale University Press, 1989) pp.xxiv-xxv.
[5] Mikhail Bakhtin, *Problems of Dostoyevsky's Poetics* (University of Minnesota

Each of these senses of poetry and methods of reading are, I hope to show, illustrative of Waldrop's own literary practice, a practice which, in relative terms, curves, which is highly attentive to the fissures, gaps, slidings, shiftings, breakages, of language, knowing, doing, being. In the words of Andrew Mossin, 'Waldrop is interested in the incoherencies, the off-key, off-balance moments of perception and experience as these get relayed in the language and form of poetry.'[6]

For Waldrop, writing corresponds to a lens, 'a frame wide enough for conjunctions and connotations. And the music of words, with its constant vanishing, to fill in the distance.'[7] Here the space of the poem is understood, quite literally, as distance. And then the aim to fill this distance not with the unseen or the invisible but with the glimpsed which disappears in sighting: the vanishing, what Waldrop terms 'a tangible emptiness.'[8] In any case, for Waldrop the poem:

> moves within language the way a dancer moves within music. Not moving through it to some destination or message. Moving within the constant disappearing and coming-into-being. With a new, fluid definition of figure and ground the way the hierarchy of the body turns fluid in dance.[9]

Orpheus turns and Eurydice is lost to him. In the instant of looking back, Eurydice vanishes. 'In this gaze, the work is lost,' but it is also one of the points at which, and by way of which, the poem begins.[10]

This is a method of reading staged as commentary, as conversation. Commentary as conversation—with texts, the processes, experiences, contradictions, of reading, thinking—becomes a series of dialogues, each in itself partial, incomplete, on the way towards, a series of snippets, snatches, responses, questions, reverberations. As Emily Carr puts it,

---

Press, 1984) p.194. I am grateful to Ben Lerner's review of Waldrop's *Curves to the Apple* for drawing my attention to this quotation. See, Ben Lerner, 'Apples of Discourse,' *Jacket* 31 (October 2006), http://jacketmagazine.com/31/lerner-waldrop.html, accessed 10 January 2012.
[6] Andrew Mossin, 'Networks of the Real in Contemporary Poetry and Poetics: Peter Middleton, Susan Schultz, Rosmarie Waldrop, *Journal of Modern Literature*, Vol. 30, No. 3 (Spring, 2007) p.150 [pp.143-153].
[7] Rosmarie Waldrop, 'The Ground is the Only Figure,' p.219.
[8] ibid, p.225.
[9] ibid, p.232.
[10] Blanchot, *The Space of Literature*, trans. Ann Smock (Lincoln and London: University of Nebraska Press, 1982) p.174.

'conversation is process-orientated; it is an experience in language.'[11] And such experiences are, always, various, fleeting, frequently circular: not a commentary, but commentaries. Just as the question of inheritance plays out across all Waldrop's writing, from private to public history, to the writings of others, the particular sense of commentary at play here corresponds to a methodological presentation of reading and writing: I want to read Waldrop's poetics but can only write about it differently, into sketch, dialogue.

Joan Retallack: 'That way of working with shorter threads, abbreviated, almost anecdotal stories, juxtaposed perceptions, a motley assortment of narrational and descriptive and linguistic units [...] creates a very different kind of world within the text than what we find in the sustained, internally coherent narrative of the more conventional novel. That form, unless it has moved from its nineteenth-century forward-thrusting track toward the "impossible" impediments and complexities of certain modernist novels, is a fully furnished panopticon, doors and windows sealed shut. The reader is led through from well-marked entrance to well-marked exit by an ever-present, entirely solicitous tour guide. Not much chance to wander and turn up things for yourself.'[12]

'Who knows,' Waldrop asks, 'what motives play into our actions. I do not know what pulls me to the place where I must, and want to, speak. Here. Where I am. "We always search for the meaning of our own life in the text we translate," says Dominique Grandmont. And sometimes we "find the other inside ourselves."'[13]

---

[11] Emily Carr, 'Happily, Revision: Reading Rosmarie Waldrop's *The Reproduction of Profiles*,' *Jacket* 36 (Late 2008), http://jacketmagazine.com/36/r-waldrop-rb-carr-emily.shtml, accessed 7 December 2011.
[12] Joan Retallack, 'A Conversation with Rosmarie Waldrop,' p.349
[13] Waldrop, *Lavish Absence*, p.151.

Relative Strangeness

All Words Are Ajar

Throughout Waldrop's connected careers as poet, translator and publisher, the world is established, tentatively, via a constant negotiation between languages, texts, cultures, histories, between forms and grammars, between familiarity and strangeness, self and other, word and silence, just as, also, it is a negotiation of those more knotty fissures between home and refuge, life and writing, matter and transcendence, tradition and innovation. As Lyn Hejinian has commented, 'language is one of the principal forms our curiosity takes. It makes us restless.'[1] In Gertrude Stein's phrase, 'the difference is spreading.'[2] Besides, as Waldrop herself comments:

> no one text has a single author in any case. The blank page is not blank. Whether we are conscious of it or not, we always write on top of a palimpsest. Like many writers, I have foregrounded this awareness of the palimpsest as a method: using, trans-forming, 'translating' parts of other works. It is not a question of linear 'influence' and not just of tradition. It is a way of getting out of myself. Into what? An interaction, a dialog with language, with a whole net of earlier and concurrent texts. Relation. Between.[3]

At issue here is an implicit foregounding in Waldrop's poetics of the importance of metonymy over metaphor. When metaphor is resisted difference spreads because differences are not rendered equivalent but contiguous. One thing leads to another and every walkway, always, is a running between.

Kornelia Freitag: 'It seems that it was just the artistic expression of the strangeness and undecidability (the "between"ness) of any culture, of any knowledge, of any language, of any experience, and of any linguistic utterance, that allowed Waldrop to write herself into the Anglo-American experimental tradition of poetry, and particularly into the anti-symbolist tradition of Gertrude Stein.'[4]

---

[1] Lyn Hejinian, 'The Rejection of Closure,' *The Language of Inquiry* (Berkeley and Los Angeles: University of California Press, 2000) p.49.
[2] Getrude Stein, *Tender Buttons* (Mineola, NY: Dover Publications, 1998) p.7.
[3] Waldrop, *Ceci*, p.91
[4] Kornelia Freitag, *Cultural Criticism in Women's Experimental Writing: The Poetry of Rosmarie Waldrop, Lyn Hejinian and Susan Howe* (Heidelberg: Universitätsverlag, 2006) p.99.

'Between' also happens to be the title of one of Waldrop's earliest poems written in English and, perhaps more than any other, it is the word that best characterises Waldrop's distinctive and highly influential approach to poetic practice over the last four decades. Hers is a poetry of betweens, of crossings, of differences and relations. 'I enter at a skewed angle,' Waldrop writes in the notebook, 'The Ground is the Only Figure,' 'through the fissures, the slight difference.'[5] As the speaker of that early poem comments, 'I'm not quite at home / on either side of the Atlantic' because 'to change your country / doesn't make you / grow':

> it doesn't make you change so much
> you can't remember
> I remember
> things are much the same
>
> so much the same the
> differences are barbed.[6]

Since the beginning Waldrop has been careful to caution against any simple conflation of poetry with biography, remarking on one occasion that 'it is not just a matter of my personal situation between countries and cultures. Our reality is no longer substances, but systems of relations.'[7]

But then, of course, neither is it easy to maintain the life and work at a permanent distance from one another. The proper relation is one of cross-tracing, a subtle and always shifting contour weaving itself between life and writing and back again. As another of Waldrop's early poems, 'For Harriet', has it:

> you can't pick out
> a thing all by itself
> each weaves together
> with the next
> inside and outside.[8]

---

[5] Waldrop, 'The Ground is the Only Figure,' p.223.
[6] Rosmarie Waldrop, *The Aggressive Ways of the Casual Stranger* (New York: Random House, 1972) p.16.
[7] Waldrop, 'Between, Always,' *Dissonance*, p.265.
[8] Waldrop, *Aggressive Ways*, p.43.

In a different register, just as no author stands alone so no text exists independently of the various lives of its author(s). So it is that, for Waldrop, poetry is frequently turned in at least two directions at once. No doubt these directions are in part primarily geographical, the result of Waldrop's relocation from Germany to America in the late 1950s. But they are also the result of the very particular way Waldrop weaves into sequence the differences between American and European traditions. Steve Evans:

> The biographical experience of linguistic dislocation not only informs Waldrop's theoretical and practical orientation toward language, it also represents a historical link to preceding generations of avant-garde writers, principally, in Waldrop's case, the Surrealists and, even more centrally, the Dadaists. Like these early writers, Waldrop engages in a literary practice predicated on a commitment to the materiality and almost plastic manipulability of language as a medium. Her own work in concrete and visual poetry in the late 1960s and early 1970s, her frequent use of collage techniques and procedural devices throughout the 1980s and 1990s, not to mention her many years of hand-setting type for Burning Deck books and chapbooks, all testify to an ongoing exploration in the fundamentally strange and surprising precincts of the material word.[9]

In various ways it is perhaps this question of inheritance—personal, historical, literary, philosophical—and specifically the manner through which it is formally traversed and engaged that maps some of the most distinctive qualities and critical engagements of Waldrop's poetry.

Waldrop is both an American poet with a continental European accent, and a European poet whose foreignness is one of her principally American characteristics.

This is so in many senses and in many manners similar to those early European émigrés who swapped tilling for tiller but who carried a cultural geography impossible to abandon in their pockets, and who built homes based on familiar customs in strange lands which inflected everything they did, so it was at once familiar and odd at the same

---

[9] Steve Evans, 'Rosmarie Waldrop,' *Dictionary of Literary Biography, vol. 169: American Poets Since WWII* (Stamford, CT: Gale, 1998); reprinted at: *Third Fiction Factory: Notes to Poetry* (2006): www.thirdfactory.net/archive_waldrop.html, accessed 19 August 2010.

time, substantial but shifting and exposed to the push and pull of the elements.

One of the most interesting ways of approaching and understanding the development of Waldrop's transatlantic poetic is in relation to the different privilege accorded the thing and the idea in Anglo-American and European poetic traditions respectively. As the critic John Taylor has commented, 'American poets tend to begin with a fact and work towards an idea, while their French counterparts begin with an idea and work toward a fact.'[10]

This Anglo-American tradition largely stems from the combined and lasting influence of Ezra Pound's mandate to 'go in fear of abstractions'[11] and William Carlos Williams' similarly direct pronouncement that there are 'no ideas but in things'.[12]

For Williams, poetry observes the tangible and, in doing so, something intangible might just emerge. It is both a practical and a seemingly authentic poetic; if the transcendental or the ineffable exists at all, it can be glimpsed only via observed reality, in those objects and actions that both surround and structure our existences.

European poetry, on the other hand, frequently leads with the abstract and, broadly speaking, is governed by what might be termed a syntactic logic. More specifically, the abstract or metaphysical approach to writing is also a primary point of differentiation between 19th century English and German realist novelists. As Martin Swales has shown, whereas English, and often French, realists treated the minutiae of social and economic life in basically secular and materialistic terms, writing in the wake of Hegel's *Lectures on Aesthetics* German writers of the nineteenth century have tended to read the phenomenal world as a cipher through which intimations of the metaphysical reveal themselves to the attentive observer. As Swales puts it, 'what that whole German tradition articulates is a sense of and feel for the complex and ceaseless interplay of materiality and mentality.'[13] Things, places, settings are sites of human signification such that they constitute a 'lining', in W.G.

---

[10] John Taylor, 'Two Cultures of the Prose Poem,' *Michigan Quarterly Review*, Vol. XLIV, No. 2, (Spring 2005), http://hdl.handle.net/2027/spo.act2080.0044.223, accessed 20 July 2012.
[11] Ezra Pound, 'A Retrospect,' *Literary Essays of Ezra Pound* (New York: New Directions, 1935) p.5.
[12] William Carlos Williams, *Paterson* (New York: New Directions, 1963) p.163.
[13] Martin Swales, 'Theoretical Reflections on the Work of W.G. Sebald,' *W.G. Sebald: A Critical Companion*, ed. J.J. Long and Anne Whitehead (Edinburgh: Edinburgh University Press, 2004) p.25.

Sebald's sense, between the physical and the metaphysical, 'materiality made eloquent by the implied "metaphysical lining."'[14]

One of the particularly striking features about Waldrop's poetry, however, is the way in which it straddles these respective traditions simultaneously, at once rooted in the tangible and leading with the ineffable. In a characteristically individual move Waldrop establishes a transatlantic poetic, one of whose primary features is the way in which her signature occupies a position somewhere in between these two different traditions. For Waldrop the ineffable is as tangible as the body she inhabits, and that body as ineffable as spirit.

'Our inclusive views,' Waldrop writes, 'are mosaics. And the shards catch light on the cut, the edges give off sparks.'[15] It is also for this reason that it is difficult to know quite where to place Waldrop: her work shares and develops many of the concerns of the post-second World War American avant-garde but at the same time it doesn't quite fit neatly into any of the critical moulds or theoretical pronouncements of American experimental poetics; similarly, Waldrop is closely connected to innovative poetries in French and German but she comes at them, despite her own German roots, at a cultural and linguistic remove. Waldrop carries this distinction into her person too. Her voice is just this side of unusual. In 1966, returning to Germany for the first time in seven years, she was greeted by her nieces' laughter. She 'talked funny':

> I had an American accent in my native language! I spoke nothing "right" any more. Even my speech marked my place between languages, between countries. My non-place.[16]

It is no surprise, then, that situated somewhere between America and Europe, one of the central axioms around which Waldrop's poetry turns is the very personal sense that language, the world, can be experienced only as gap or aperture, the stutter of syntax. 'I enter [language] at a skewed angle', Waldrop writes in the essay 'Thinking of Follows', through the fissures, the slight difference.'[17] Or again:

> The linguistic displacement from German to English has not only made me into a translator, but has given me a sense of writing as exploration of what happens between; between

---

[14] Swales, 'Theoretical Reflections on the Work of W.G. Sebald,' p.28.
[15] Waldrop, *Ceci*, pp.18-19.
[16] ibid, p.79.
[17] Waldrop, 'Thinking of Follows,' *Dissonance*, p.208.

words, sentences, people, cultures. In writing, this of course means composition. I am not so much concerned with the 'right word,' but how words connect, their affinities, slidings, the gaps between, the shadow zone of silence and margins. As Gertrude Stein knew from the start: 'Everything is the same except composition and as the composition is different and always going to be different everything is not the same.'[18]

So it is that not everything can be explained away. Even as it is laid out and made material across the page, Waldrop's poetry might be said to be always disappearing elsewhere, moving off at a grammatical tangent, the specificity of its language deviating in a direction difficult to follow and still harder to arrest. As Maurice Blanchot puts it: '*There was something like a word that could not be pronounced, even when one succeeded in saying it and perhaps because one had, at every instant, and as if there were not enough instants for the purpose, to say it, to think it.*'[19]

It is this instant in which Waldrop is most interested. Or, more accurately, that actual between-point the instant gives onto, those stubborn planes Wittgenstein calls 'imponderable evidence' and which include, among other things, 'subtleties of glance, of gesture, of tone.'[20] Something does not give, necessarily, and cannot. The intricacies that condition any statement may be never fully independently verified, that is, they could never be appraised—pondered—via recourse to any general principle or universal law. Gilles Deleuze: '*When a language is so strained* that it starts to stutter, or to murmur or stammer ... *then language in its entirety reaches the limit* that marks its outside and makes it confront silence. When a language is strained in this way, language in its entirety is submitted to a pressure that makes it fall silent.'[21]

'When Waldrop says she doesn't have thoughts,' writes Joan Retallack, 'she has methods that make language think, she is referring to a similar movement away from grammars of inertia. Waldrop turns her own restlessness and anxiety of insufficiency into a navigational project, a poetics of formal choices that throw text into motion as life processes themselves. This has to do with material energies of language—vocabularies, syntaxes, juxtaposition dynamics, interpretive

---

[18] Waldrop, 'Thinking of Follows,' p.208.
[19] Maurice Blanchot, *The Step Not Beyond*, trans. Lycette Nelson (Albany, NY: State University of New York Press, 1992) p.103.
[20] Ludwig Wittgenstein, *Philosophical Investigations* (Oxford: Blackwell, 2009) p.237.
[21] Gilles Deleuze, 'He Stuttered,' *Essays Critical and Clinical*, trans. Daniel W. Smith and Michael A. Greco (London and New York: Verso, 1998) p.113.

coordinates.'[22]

And yet none of this should be taken to suggest that Waldrop's poetry is esoteric—her poems may be made up of complex layers but there is always a clear and considered process guiding her poetic methods. If, on occasion, her work can appear difficult it is simply because she is concerned not with recording impressions but with reflecting surfaces—'all the depths that lie in the bright, fragile surface of things' in Hoffmansthal's phrase—and showing how one thing connects to another and making method that often strange relation.[23] As Wittgenstein knew, it is difficult to describe something or someone without attributing to the details our own take on things. 'Indeed, often,' Wittgenstein says, 'I can describe [someone's] inner, as I perceive it, but not his outer.'[24] Likewise it can be difficult to read words on a page and not between the lines. It's even harder perhaps to get out of ourselves and simply transcribe the ground we're standing on.

Wittgenstein has been an important influence on Waldrop's writing for many years. The reasons for Waldrop's particular interest in Wittgenstein are various. On a primary, level, this influence and connection is related to the ways in which the philosopher's project in the *Tractatus* of relating the logical form of 'the world' to 'the logic of language' resonates closely with Waldrop's work. Most particularly, though, Wittgenstein stands out for Waldrop because his method so closely approximates Waldrop's own concerns in her poetry. In other words, the logical method of the philosopher is reflected in the poetics of the writer who questions, analyses, and subsequently revises.

In refutation of his earlier systematic theory of language, as exemplified by *Tractatus*, in his later writings, and in particular in *The Blue and Brown Book*, Wittgenstein's central arguments are frequently couched in figurative discourse, especially through the use of similes, metaphors, and analogies. As Sue-Im Lee notes, this 'analogy-driven process of argument (e.g., language is like "a game of chess," using language is like "playing chess" or like "performing a transaction"; "use" is like "meaning" and like "understanding"; etc.) rests on an array of examples, and each example gives rise to a proliferation of possible

---

[22] Joan Retallack, 'A Conversation with Rosmarie Waldrop,' p.335.
[23] Hugo von Hoffmannsthal, 'The Lord Chandos Letter' in *The Whole Difference: Selected Writings of Hugo von Hoffmannsthal*, ed. J.D. McClatchy (Princeton, NJ: Princeton University Press, 2008) p.17.
[24] Ludwig Wittgenstein, *Last Writings on the Philosophy of Psychology: The Inner and the Outer*, vol.2 (Oxford: Blackwell, 1992) p.62.

interpretations.'[25] In many senses, it is precisely this proliferation that draws Waldrop to Wittgenstein, and in particular, to working creatively or procedurally with his method.

David Antin draws a parallel between this philosophical and poetic method by suggesting the ways in which such a practice has various affinities with the scope and general consequence of literary collage: 'collage involves suppression of the ordering signs that would specify the 'stronger logical relations' among the presented elements. By "stronger logical relations" I mean relations of implication, entailment, negation, subordination and so on. Among logical relations that may still be present are relations of similarity, equivalence, identity, their negative forms, dissimilarity, nonequivalence, nonidentity, and some kind of image of concatenation, grouping or association.'[26]

As Waldrop puts it in the essay 'Velocity but no location', 'it's difficult to realize the groundlessness of our beliefs, but my style is fragmentary in any case, and my life as perplexed as my writing.'[27] It is also for this reason that Waldrop maintains 'language is not a tool for me, but a medium infinitely larger than my intention. What will find resonance is out of my hands.'[28] It is out of Waldrop's hands precisely because, as her writing repeatedly attests, in themselves 'all words are ajar', all words open onto a curvature of space and so are held in strange relation: 'an art of separation and fusion, of displacement and connection [...] An art of betweens.'[29]

Detour is a method of approach as good as any. 'All words are ajar;' all writing opens onto the space of something other than itself. As one of the sections from the sequence 'As If We Didn't Have to Talk,' taken from Waldrop's first published collection, *The Aggressive Ways of the Casual Stranger*, puts it, 'the road just / goes on / without asking / for approval / opaque pulsations.'[30]

---

[25] Sue-Im Lee, *A Body of Individuals: The Paradox of Community in Contemporary Fiction* (Columbus, OH: The Ohio State University Press, 2009) p.179, n.4.
[26] David Antin, '"Some Questions about Modernism," *Occident*, 8 (Spring 1974): 7-38.
[27] Rosmarie Waldrop, 'Velocity but no location,' *Salt Magazine*, Issue 2 (April 2008) n.p.
[28] Waldrop, 'Thinking of Follows,' p.208.
[29] Rosmarie Waldrop, 'Between, Always,' *Dissonance*, p.273.
[30] Waldrop, *The Aggressive Ways of the Casual Stranger*, p.69.

'To Peel Off Childhood Like So Many Skins'[1]

Rosmarie Waldrop was born on 24 August 1935 in Kitzingen am Main, the third daughter to parents Josef and Friederike Sebald.

All towns have their own slough. And Kitzingen, it would appear, is no different. A medium-sized town of around 21,000 inhabitants, Kitzingen is situated in north-west Bavaria, Germany. According to legend, Kitzingen was founded around 750 when an unnamed daughter of King Pippin the Short (714-768; son of Charles Martel, subsequent Mayor of the Palace and then, later, King of the Franks) dropped a scarf from the ramparts of Schwanberg castle. And so it went that:

> the wind carried the bit of cloth down the mountain side, played with it, tossed it up, flouting superior strength, and then unclenched its grip, letting the lacy butterfly sag and fall. Down by the river, the Main, shepherd Kitz found it crumpled and soggy with dew.[2]

Under the authority of St Boniface, St. Adelheid, the first Abbess of Kitzingen, is said to have built the town's Benedictine monastery on the exact spot where Kitz, chilled in the damp of the day, stooped to gather in the scarf and tied it, squarely, about his chest.

Reliable records are hard to come by and the importance of Kitzingen's monastery appears to have fallen into decline following the death of its second abbess, the English missionary, St Thecla, around 790 AD. Between 1440 and 1629 Kitzingen was mortgaged to the margraves of Brandenburg. During the Peasants War of 1525 the tombs of St. Adelheid and St. Thecla were profaned when a local advocate of Lutheran reformation used their heads to play at skittles.[3] In 1629 the town was purchased by Philip Adolphus, Bishop of Würzburg, and the monastery restored as school for the Ursulines. Following three years of Swedish occupation during the Thirty Years War, in 1650 displaced Protestants were encouraged to return under Bishop Johann Philip von Schoenborn of Würzburg's Edict of Toleration. The subsequent growth of the town's population combined with its profitable location resulted

---

[1] Rosmarie Waldrop, *Split Infinites* (Philadelphia, PA: Singing Horse Press, 1998), p.50.
[2] Rosmarie Waldrop, *The Hanky of Pippin's Daughter* (Evanston, IL: Northwestern University Press, 2000) p.101.
[3] 'St. Thecla,' *Catholic Encyclopaedia*, http://www.newadvent.org/cathen/14563a.htm, accessed 8 August 2010.

in Kitzingen becoming an important economic centre on the Main River, particularly for the trade of locally produced wine, as well as the distribution of fruit, grain and timber. It was this wine workers are said to have used in the mortar when constructing the town's leaning landmark, the *Falterturm*, during a drought in the 13th century.

Following Napoleon's abolition of the Holy Roman Empire, in 1814 Kitzingen was annexed to the Kingdom of Bavaria, becoming part of the newly formed German Empire in 1871. In 1917 Kitzingen Army Airfield was built two miles from the centre of town and used as a training school for German pilots in World War I. Between the wars the land was returned to local farmers although by the time of Waldrop's birth the airfield was once again being used as a military training academy, this time of Luftwaffe bomber and pursuit squadrons. With the outbreak of the Second World War Waldrop's father, Josef, became a 'flying instructor with the rank of captain.'[4] After several bombing raids by the US Air Force the Luftwaffe abandoned the airfield in April 1945. The airfield became a garrison of the US Air Force for two years before becoming a US Army occupation garrison in 1947, and then being turned into the Harvey and Larson Barracks in 1951. Both facilities were closed and returned to the German government in March 2007. Today, Kitzingen's main industries are brewing, cask-making and the manufacture of cement and colours.

In spite of this history, to all intents and purposes Waldrop's early childhood was comfortably middle class and Christian. Josef Sebald taught physical education at the local high school and Friederike was an accomplished amateur singer with an attachment to opera and the patina of society. Despite the stewardship of Freiderike's Prussian Protestantism in the day to day running of the household, the Sebald's three daughters were brought up under the aegis of their father's Catholicism. But Sebald was a man of his age and lived with a national sense of crisis and cultural nihilism following Germany's collapse after the First World War. In attitude of therapeutic restoration, Sebald's Catholicism grew increasingly idiosyncratic, tempered by what Waldrop describes as his pantheistic naturalism and his interest in astrology ('Father went to mass on Sundays, but his real church was the forest, his religion a mix of pantheism and astrology', as Waldrop puts it in *Ceci n'est pas Rosmarie*),[5] but which might as equally be thought

---
[4] Waldrop, *The Hanky*, p.138.
[5] Waldrop, *Ceci*, p.70.

of along the lines of Heidegger's contemporaneous holism and sense of 'geschichte' or 'deep history.'

For Heidegger, deep history corresponds to his hopes for a German renewal by engaging in a thorough critique of the bases of Western history. By deep history, in other words, Heidegger meant that life source of energy or spirit which might be mobilised in service of national recovery, and which Heidegger saw particularly exemplified in Georg Trakl's poetry, describing it as being 'historical in the highest [deepest] sense' in that it 'sings of the destiny which casts humankind forward into its still withheld nature, thereby saving or salvaging the latter.'[6] Heidegger's chief concern was with productionist metaphysics, in other words, that branch of Western history which has understood politics as a craft and has linked that 'craft' with the making or fashioning of a people according to some such idea or ideal of community. Timothy Clark stresses the ways in which this sense of politics intensified the association of politics with craft, noting how Nazism 'stressed the genuine essence of Germany as something the German people should continuously create, in their daily life and activities, all of which in turn became celebrated as the expression of a common essence and destiny.'[7] This destiny is made manifest in flags, uniforms, insignia, habits, customs, political rallies, propaganda. Against this, Heidegger aimed to take the terms of Western life back to their Greek sources and by so doing to open the space for a new beginning. 'The beginning *exists* still,' Heidegger stressed. 'It does not lie *behind* us, as something long past, but it stands *before* us' as a task, a challenge, a demand.[8] This return to deep history, Heidegger believed, had the potential to alter, fundamentally and profoundly, the most basic attitudes and assumptions governing the world. For Heidegger, such a project of renewal was about aiming to overcome what he saw as the cultural and political nihilism of the age, but it was a project which also found its more generalised and more dangerous but contemporaneous political echo in Hitler's 'Let Germany awaken and renew her strength, let her remember her greatness and recover her old position in the world.'[9]

---

[6] Martin Heidegger, 'Language in the Poem,' *On the Way to Language*, trans. Peter D. Hertz (San Francisco, CA: Harper & Row, 1971) p.196.
[7] Timothy Clark, *Martin Heidegger* (London: Routledge, 2002) p.127.
[8] Martin Heidegger, 'The Self-Assertion of the German University,' trans. William S. Lewis, in Wolin (ed.), *The Heidegger Controversy: A Critical Reader* (Cambridge, MA: MIT Press, 1993) p.32.
[9] Quoted in *The Hanky*, p.122.

And just as, for a brief time at least, Heidegger saw the possibility of this renewal in Germany in the early 1930s, so Josef Sebald also perceived the possibility of national and spiritual renewal embedded within, at the very least, the early expression of the Nazi project.

Inevitably, then, Waldrop's childhood was marked in decisive manner by the cultural ordinariness and homeliness, relatively speaking, of National Socialism and the voice of Hitler again and again marching its way out of the radio. Nazi Germany was not an aberration that went on elsewhere but was part of the Sebald's domestic landscape, and actively so: if the various references in Waldrop's writing are accurate, Waldrop's parents and their friends were staunch supporters of National Socialism, Josef Sebald consolidating this support when, in 1932, one year before membership became compulsory for anyone concerned with maintaining their employment, he joined the Nazi Party.[10] 'To know that I have come out of this,' Waldrop comments much later in interview.[11] But a child, necessarily, takes it for granted their parents' world is discerning and right. 'And then war came out of the radio before I had time.'[12]

That National Socialism was simply part of the texture of everyday life was reinforced when Waldrop went to school in 1941. 'War internalized as everything.'[13] As Waldrop puts it in *Split Infinites* and repeats with only very slight modification in her autobiography:

> My first schoolday, September 1941, a cool day. Time did not pass, but was conducted to the brain. I was taught. The Nazi salute, the flute. How firmly entrenched, the ancient theories. Already using paper, pen, ink. Yes, I said, I'm here.[14]

There are clear autobiographical experiences being registered here but the real resonance of a passage like this is, I think, in its banality. Tradition and custom are the habit of the classroom and belonging is the child's reward for declaring herself present.

In 1943, when Waldrop was eight, Kitzingen was bombed:

> When we climbed out of the cellar there were no streets, no rows of houses. Instead: craters, heaps of rubble, mortar,

---

[10] Waldrop discusses this most explicitly in *The Hanky*, p.122.
[11] Retallack, 'A Conversation,' p. 341.
[12] Waldrop, *Split Infinites*, p.62.
[13] ibid, p.60.
[14] ibid, p.58.

stones, walls broken off, a craggy desert, air thick with dust. A few houses were left standing. They seemed out of place, incongruous with their insistence on boundaries, definite lines. Then came two years of being shifted from village to village, from parents to acquaintances to relatives.[15]

Waldrop refers to this as 'the first drastic change of my world.' A second followed in 1945 when, '"Our leader" turned into "the criminal," "the enemy" into "Amis" [short for Americans], "surrender" into "liberation." This went deeper and took years to understand.'[16] In fact, it took Waldrop until the 1980s to begin to broach this period of her life in her writing, first with the semi-fictionalised but oblique—Waldrop refers to it as 'at best a small periplus along an edge'[17]—account in *The Hanky of Pippin's Daughter* (whose 152 pages took Waldrop eight years to complete) and then, in 1992, with the prose poem sequence 'Split Infinites'. In part, this was because Waldrop's post-war resumption of childhood coincided with concerted attempts to shelter the young from the actual facts of National Socialism. Thus, Waldrop notes, 'history classes did not go up to the Nazi period' and 'few parents [were] willing to talk about it.'[18]

But Waldrop's difficulty in broaching her familial past was also the result of something more personally rooted and complex. As Waldrop knew, 'we could not distance ourselves and say "they." *We* had done this, *our* country.'[19] The complexity of this legacy was compounded by Waldrop's own sense that, had the war in Europe continued for only another few months, she, like her sisters before her, would have been drafted into the Hitler Youth on the occasion of her tenth birthday. The difficult question such awareness posed for Waldrop concerned how she would have acted in that situation. In other words, would she, like her parents and sisters, have gone along with it by conforming, have obediently raised her hand at the sound of her name and said, 'Yes, I'm here'? As Waldrop notes, 'heroism is the exception; most human beings are not cut out for it.'[20]

---

[15] Waldrop, 'Between, Always,' p.269.
[16] Waldrop, *Ceci*, p.63.
[17] Waldrop, 'The Ground is the Only Figure,' p.219.
[18] Waldrop, *Ceci*, p.66.
[19] ibid, p.67.
[20] ibid, p.67.

Music Was Everywhere

Following the end of the war and after a brief period spent among the ruins with a travelling theatre troupe, touring towns and villages playing a dwarf in *Snow White* in the afternoons and Enyusha, a nobleman's son, in Wedekind's *Love Potion* in the evenings, Waldrop returned to school in 1946. Things settled down to normal. There were bickers and silences at home, the usual frustrations of a family and one roof, the refuge of reading and the elsewhere. Many chairs space a life. Games were played outside, next to a stretch of untended yard behind Kumor's print shop, 'among the slabs of limestone leaning upright against the wall. Each slab showed the negative of the wine labels that had been printed from it' and the smell of inks and solvent hung in the air.[1]

Adolescence met with a growing quietness, uncertainties of the body and of behaviour felt even more acutely by forays into charm and dance. Music was everywhere: piano, flute, a mother in song, a youth orchestra; each and every experience 'multiplied into many instances of speculation.'[2] And music, like any field at once constitutive and unknown, coming from a long way off, 'coming, perhaps deceptively, as also the beginning of all music' where something disappears and appears 'without our being able to decide between apparition and disappearance.'[3] In the evenings, 'Mother lit candles and kerosene lamps.'[4]

By 1954 Waldrop had enrolled to study Comparative Literature at the University of Würzburg, taking classes in literature, art history and musicology. Waldrop was also still playing piano and flute in a local youth orchestra. That Christmas, the orchestra performed a concert for the American soldiers occupying Kitzingen's nearby army bases. The orchestra was better attended than the audience but it was here that Rosmarie met the then serving American private, Keith Waldrop.

Keith Waldrop (*né* Bernard Waldrop; Keith is his middle name) was born 11 December 1932 in Emporia, Kansas, son of a railroad worker father and an itinerant piano teacher mother, and raised in an environment of comics, the Bible and amateur invention. According to Keith, his father claimed to have invented the refrigerator (if only Lord Kelvin had been slower registering the patent), attempted to produce a

---

[1] Waldrop, 'The Ground is the Only Figure,' p.246.
[2] Waldrop, *Split Infinites*, p.50.
[3] Blanchot, *Friendship*, p.116.
[4] Waldrop, *Split Infinites*, p.52.

synthetic rubber from Osage apples and patented a self-wringing mop, 'with a mechanism so complicated as to preclude production.'[5] A pre-med student of psychiatry at Kansas State Teachers College, in 1953 Waldrop was drafted and sent as an army engineer in water purification to Germany. And so it is all of a sudden tendons can tense and all life suddenly appear to be snapped into direction: 'you feel a splinter and know where it came from.'[6] For the four months following the concert until Keith's army discharge, the Waldrops-to-be met weekly to listen to records and, in what would prove to be the beginning of a collaborative process that has remained at the centre of their respective careers ever since, translate poems from German into English, the first of these being Nietzsche's 'Tanzlied' from *Thus Spoke Zarathustra* which dramatises a moment of keen awakening and recognition and which contains the lines: 'Gladly would I walk with thee – in some lovelier place! / In the paths of love, through bushes variegated, quiet, trim! Or there along the lake, where gold-fishes dance and swim!' and: 'all pleasure wants eternity.'[7]

Towards the end of 1954 Keith returned to America. It may well be that 'day follows day with the certainty initiated by the rotary press' but a body is often predisposed for movement and can go off elsewhere all the while leaving an impression, tangible and incontestable.[8] The following academic year Rosmarie transferred to the University of Freiburg 'to avoid living at home' and came across Robert Musil's monumental modernist novel *The Man Without Qualities*, published between 1930 and 1942.[9] The discovery of Musil would have long-lasting consequences.

For Waldrop it was the kaleidoscopic reach of Musil's ideas that made his work resonate. In particular, it was Musil's non-literariness, the ways in which his writing attempts to blend the abstract with the tangible in a manner distinctly different to other modernist contemporaries, such as James Joyce and Marcel Proust. As Burton Pike comments, 'Musil looked at the world from the viewpoint of a scientific philosopher; he was concerned with analysing and criticising the world as it is, and he was more interested in ideas and actions. His talent, in other words,

---

[5] Waldrop, *Ceci*, p.13.
[6] Waldrop, *Split Infinites*, p.54.
[7] Friedrich Nietzsche, *Thus Spake Zarathustra*, trans. Thomas Common (Ware: Wordsworth Editions, 1997) p.354.
[8] Waldrop, *Split Infinites*, p.68.
[9] Waldrop, *Ceci*, p.71.

was analytic and conceptual rather than conceptual and dramatic.'[10] An entry from Musil's diary in 1910 is equally revealing. 'What I care about,' Musil wrote, 'is the passionate energy of thought. Where I can't work out some particular thought, work becomes immediately boring to me; this is true of almost every single paragraph.'[11]

As well as a sense of intellectual affinity, Waldrop was fascinated also by Musil's particular method of narrative fragmentation, specifically his use in *The Man Without Qualities* of discrete narrative fragments or units which exhibit neither a consistent nor a unifying pattern. 'There is an openness,' Waldrop has commented of Musil in interview, 'a grid structure that allows great complexity, a nonlinear narrative [...] When he gives you a narrative line it is in ironical juxtaposition with a grid or web structure.'[12] At all times, narrative thread is questioned and frustrated. Digressions and detail take over and focus is fractal. Or as Waldrop explains in the essay 'Thinking of Follows,' fragmentation allows the poet 'to frustrate the expectation of continuity, of step-by-step-linearity.'[13] There is, Waldrop suggests:

> a kind of orchestral meaning that comes about in the break [of linearity], a vertical dimension made up of the energy field between the two lines (or phrases or sentences). A meaning that both connects and illuminates the gap, so that the shadow zone of silence between the elements gains weight, becomes an element of the structure.[14]

This issue of the nonlinear narrative is central. As Joan Retallack has put it:

> If logical systems are, as Kurt Gödel tells us, inherently incomplete; if mass *is* energy, particle *is* wave, space *is* time, and vice versa; if natural and cultural histories are chaotic, if complex surfaces *are* fractal (allowing infinite detail to exist within finite space-time delineations) then the question arises, What is implied about the forms with which we attempt to make meaning out of our experience?[15]

---

[10] Burton Pike, *Robert Musil: An Introduction to His Work* (Port Washington, N.Y., and London: Kennikat Press, 1972) p.1.
[11] Robert Musil, quoted in Pike, p.2
[12] Joan Retallack, 'A Conversation,' pp.354 and 361.
[13] Waldrop, 'Thinking of Follows,' p.211.
[14] ibid, p.210.
[15] Joan Retallack, *op. cit.*, p.331-2.

Within such a context *The Man Without Qualities* can be understood as a kaleidoscopic narrative marked by a sense, variously conceived, of loss, atomisation, and breakdown: cultural, political, moral, and personal. In Musil this sense of the modern is most clearly registered through the representation of the world as without unity. For Musil, in other words, there appears to be no sense of a schema or process of systematisation that would be capable of arresting this accelerating process of fragmentation and non-equivalence that, for him, characterises modern experience. As Musil has the central character, Ulrich, explain:

> What puts our minds at rest is the simple sequence, the overwhelming variegation of life now represented in, as a mathematician would say, a unidimensional order: the stringing upon one thread of all that has happened in space and time, in short, that notorious 'narrative thread' of which it then turns out the thread of life itself consists.[16]

The point, though, is that it is this sense of sequence or 'narrative thread' that, Musil suggests, modern experience disavows. As a result, and in lines that follow the passage quoted above, Ulrich observes how he appears to have 'lost this elementary narrative element' and that 'everything now has become non-narrative, no longer following a "thread," but spreading out an infinitely interwoven surface.'[17] As Gertrude Stein knew so well, 'the whole business of writing is living one's contemporariness.' And the 'thing that is important is that nobody knows what the contemporariness is. In other words, they don't know where they are going, but they are on their way.'[18] Or, as Musil put it in a diary entry, 'everything becomes for me fragments of a theoretical system. But I have given up philosophy, thus there is no justification for it. There remain only: illuminations.'[19] In Waldrop these illuminations become the shards of one of the most important aesthetic concepts in her writing, namely, the 'between'.

In certain respects, the atomisation of language and life in Musil's novel is greeted with a certain nostalgia, a general pervasive feeling of loss. This general condition of loss is perhaps most clearly illustrated

---

[16] Robert Musil, *The Man Without Qualities, Vol. II, The Like of It Now Happens* (London: Secker & Warburg, 1953) p.436.
[17] ibid, p.436.
[18] Gertrude Stein, *How Writing is Written* (Los Angeles: Black Sparrow, 1974) p.19.
[19] Robert Musil, quoted in Pike, *Robert Musil*, p.5.

in the scene when the cultural and moral perspective of the novel's great industrialist and popular philosopher, Arnheim, is overwhelmed by the 'feeling that he had forgotten some path he had originally been following, and that the whole of the ideology of the great man (with which he had been fulfilled) was only the emergency substitute for something he had lost.'[20] Yet even though such statements would appear to imply a wider nostalgia for a previous age—idealised, imagined, actual, or otherwise—the specific structural form and compositional method of Musil's novel, with its combination of narrative, essay, and commentary, opens the door for other readings and possibilities of the so-called non-narrative.

For Waldrop, what particularly stands out from this compositional strategy is the conception of the book, rather than the chapter, or the scene, or the paragraph, or even the sentence, as organising unit. The book becomes a kaleidoscope of pieces, diversions, shards; the specific interplay between those discrete units only becomes clear, or does not, at the book's end; here the whole corresponds to the division rather than the sum of its parts. *The Man Without Qualities* is a massive piece of work, but it is one which, ultimately, is a mass of pieces as much about its structure and its making—about the impossibility of its completion, about the limits and the possibilities of the book—as anything else. As Burton Pike puts it, Musil's novel is 'an open rather than a closed system of thought, a search on the border of the impossible for new directions of moral development. The basic moral question is how to live; this question is at the center of the work.'[21] Indeed, despite the slightly old-fashioned register of Pike's point here, his general argument sheds light on an important impulse and urgency that runs throughout Waldrop's various publications, and it is one which finds its formative origins in the example of Musil. As Waldrop puts it in her autobiography:

> Musil's concept of identity rang true to me: consisting of multiple selves, with 'character' and 'qualities' being our most impersonal traits because they are what is reinforced from the outside. And I was fascinated by the way the narrative calls itself into question, both thematically and by always pitting a two-dimensional grid of details against the famous 'narrative thread'. This became important for my own method

---

[20] Musil, *The Man Without Qualities*, Vol. II, p.97.
[21] Pike, *Robert Musil*, p.24

of composition: the tension between clusters (lines or single words) scattered on a page and a temporal sequence.[22]

This question—aesthetic, moral, philosophical, political—of an open system, what Waldrop referencing Creeley usually refers to as 'multiple intersections *around* which' rather than a 'container *within* which,' cuts to the recurrent centre of Waldrop's poetic project in all its various guises.[23] As Waldrop comments in interview, 'I always have multiplicity, scatter, and must search for the jelling point, the point of intersection, something fluid, but with cohesion.'[24] Over time, that point of fluid cohesion increasingly becomes the scene and space of the book itself, such that the book as both ground and form—first demonstrated by Musil and later influentially developed by Jabès—increasingly becomes one of the central compositional principles behind Waldrop's work. It does so because it emblematises one of Waldrop's chief aims, namely the attempt to see these things as they appear, a various assemblage composed of different units, pieces, phrases, fragments, interleaved, juxtaposed, such that the aim is to see things how they may be, perhaps, or how they fall through the gaps, catch the light in the spaces between.

---

[22] Waldrop, *Ceci*, p.72.
[23] Retallack, 'A Conversation,' p.370.
[24] ibid, p.353.

'Since I Cannot Put the World to Rights, I Speak of Love'[1]

The year of Waldrop's discovery of Musil was also the year Germany began to grow an army again.

GI Bills and study-abroad programmes can be passports alike and Keith Waldrop and Rosmarie Sebald spent 1956-57 studying together at the University of Aix-Marseille. In 1958, Keith entered three Hopwood contests at the University of Michigan. The Hopwood Programme was the legacy of former student and dramatist, Avery Hopwood. Begun in 1931 the awards are designed to promote and support creative work in writing. Keith Waldrop entered 'with three manuscripts: one poetry, one fiction and, for the essay contest, an old seminar paper. My poetry got nothing. My fiction got nothing. The seminar paper won.'[2] The prize was $600—enough for Rosmarie's passage from Germany to America with a little left over to cover living expenses. With a place waiting for her on the graduate programme in comparative literature at the University of Michigan in Ann Arbor, on 17 December 1958 Waldrop set sail aboard the slow boat for America. By Waldrop's account, 'it was a rough crossing. The boat took eleven days instead of the scheduled ten. I was seasick during five of them and swore never to set foot on a ship again.'[3] One month later, having received Josef Sebald's permission after his consultation with an astrologer on the matter, Rosmarie and Keith were married by Catholic service.

In America steps lead out of the way to where books and examples remarked centuries turning and other lines of thinking. By day, a flock of birds, threshing tinder, and by night, hands peaked as envelope, folding resolutely, just as the consequence of body is change. Waldrop listened, a way of waiting, turned toward the world, the first buds, the smelt of type behind and ahead. All that was figure now ground, 'the way a mirror gets behind the subject.'[4]

Waldrop recalls her first bus ride after arriving in the United States, from New York to Michigan, a long journey of 500 or so miles, travelling in a slight north-westerly direction: 'The feeling of SPACE, of

---

[1] John Gower, *Confessio*, Book 1, quoted in Michael Schmidt, *Lives of the Poets* (New York: Knopf, 1999) p.41.
[2] Waldrop. *Ceci*, p.17
[3] ibid, p.72.
[4] Waldrop, *Split Infinites*, p.91.

relatively wild space, of woods going on and on was overwhelming to me. Space in Germany is so much more cramped, hemmed in, every inch of ground husbanded.'[5] Waldrop identified with Olson's sense of America as space and movement, with which he begins his 1947 work, *Call Me Ishmael*:

> I take SPACE to be the central fact to man born in America, from Folsom cave to now. I spell it large because it comes large here. Large and without mercy.
>
> It is geography at bottom, a hell of wide land from the beginning. That made the first American story (Parkman's): exploration.
>
> Something else than a stretch of earth—seas on both sides, no barriers to contain as restless a thing as Western man was becoming in Columbus' day.[6]

'You might say,' Waldrop adds, that such ideas are 'a natural site for a poetics of metonymy, of horizontal expansion,' before she again quotes Olson's sense of the 'figure of outward.'[7]

In Michigan Waldrop discovered a circle of writers, musicians and artists—including James Camp, Don Hope, Dallas Wiebe, Nelson Howe, John Heath-Stubbs and X.J. Kennedy[8]—bound by a shared interest in and enthusiasm for modernist literary and aesthetic experiment. Most importantly, though, this was a group of people who, spurred on by one another's enthusiasms, were putting their ideas about poetry into practice and doing it for themselves. And it was out of this endeavour that the Waldrops' groundbreaking and highly influential press, Burning Deck, was established, the first title—edited by Hope and including work by the then notorious Donald Hall, as well as W.D. Snodgrass, Kennedy, Wiebe, Camp, Heath-Stubbs and Keith—being published in 1961.

Time passes and feet take their paths. In 1964 the Waldrops moved from Michigan to Wesleyan, Connecticut and from there, in 1968, to

---

[5] Cooperman, Matthew Cooperman, 'Between Tongues: An Interview with Rosmarie Waldrop,' *Conjunctions* (2005), http://www.conjunctions.com/webcon/cooperman.htm, accessed 8 August 2012.
[6] Charles Olson, *Call Me Ishmael* (Baltimore and London: The Johns Hopkins University Press, 1967) p.11.
[7] Matthew Cooperman, *op. cit.*
[8] Between 1962 and 1965 Don Hope co-edited *Burning Deck* magazine with Keith Waldrop.

Providence, Rhode Island, and then to 71 Elmgrove Avenue, the house which has been their home ever since. Rhode Island is the smallest state in area in the United States, and the first of the original colonies to declare independence from British rule, on May 4, 1776. Providence was founded in 1636 by the breakaway Christian liberalist Roger Williams as a refuge for those whom he termed the 'distressed of conscience.'[9] Williams had challenged the Puritan doctrine of theocracy, calling for a separation of church and state on the grounds that a civil state had no jurisdiction over the consciences of individuals. When Williams then challenged the legitimacy of the Puritan setters' title to the land in 1632 with a treatise arguing that the a royal charter did not entitle English colonists to Indian land, he was tried for political heresy, banished from Massachusetts for 300 years, and had his treatise burned.

As Waldrop reports it, an attempt was made to deport Williams to England, 'but he was forewarned and fled to an Indian settlement on the east bank of the Seekonk river.'[10] Writing in his journal on 11 January 1636, John Winthrop, the first governor of 'The Company of Massachusetts Bay in New England,' goes into a little more detail, noting how the Bay consulate discussed the case of Roger Williams and decided to have him deported by boat to England for continuing to preach and entertain people in his house 'notwithstanding the injunction laid upon him.' A warrant, Winthrop states, was sent to Williams, demanding that he come to Boston.

> He returned answer (and divers of Salem came with it) that he could not come without hazard of his life, etc., whereupon a pinnace was sent with commission to Captain Underhill, etc., to apprehend him and carry him aboard the ship (when then at Nantasket), but when they came at his house they found he had been gone 3 days before, but wither they could not learn.[11]

Once Williams had crossed the Seekonk river, he purchased land from the Native American Pokanoket Tribe of the Wampanoag Nation and named the settlement Providence, 'in grateful remembrance of

---

[9] James D. Knowles, *Memoir of Roger Williams, the Founder of the State of Rhode Island* (Boston, MA: Lincoln Edmands and Co., 1834), p.103.
[10] Waldrop, 'A Key into the Key,' *Dissonance*, p.192.
[11] John Winthrop, *The Journal of John Winthrop, 1630-1649*, ed. Richard S. Dunn and Laetitia Yeandle (Harvard: John Harvard Library, 1996); quoted in *The Norton Anthology of American Literature, Vol. A*, 8th edition, ed. Wayne Franklin (New York and London: Norton, 2012) p.179.

God's merciful providence to him in distress.'[12] He lived by farming and trade with the Indians.

Rhode Island became a refuge for those who found themselves on the margins of the Massachusetts Bay society: Separatists, Baptists, Seekers, Antinomians, Jews, and Quakers all found a home there. In 1663 Rhode Island received a royal charter from Charles II in which freedom of conscience was guaranteed. As has been well documented, this was something of which not even Englishman at the time were assured, and 'it became so indelibly "American" an idea that provision was made for it in the 1791 Bill of Rights.'[13]

In 1643 Williams published the first study of the Amerindian language in English, *A Key into the Language of America*. Over the years, both Rosmarie and Keith have repeatedly engaged with the colonial origins of Providence, most explicitly in Rosmarie's reworking of Williams' *A Key into the Language of America* (1994), and Keith in *The Quest for Mount Misery* (1983).

'The years in Providence,' Waldrop writes, 'seem round, filling the whole space. Like whales, in smooth hipless motion. Simple time open toward quiet, persistent love, friends, reading, writing. Black dots across the screen. To pinpoint events not as easy as in the times abroad, memories keyed to place.'[14] Time opens out and a place takes on other shapes, familiar, and comforting, and a life finds itself reflected in geography. As Keith Waldrop puts it, 'What is in my mind—or I should simply say, what my mind is (which is to say, my environment)—well, in a sense, that is precisely what I'm not.' And yet, as Waldrop goes on to add, 'in another sense, it is all in the world I am.'[15]

For many years, this world, this environment, has been synonymous with the Waldrops' home at 71 Elmgrove Avenue. As Rosmarie puts it, '71 Elmgrove Avenue is nearly a century old. Old for this country. There are no elms left on Elmgrove Avenue. Maples. Water seeps into the basement. The wind sets the wood creaking, the walls crack where they've been forced to meet. When I roll a marble along the floor for the cat, its path maps the most unpredictable slopes and valleys.'[16] Just so the course of a body, a mind, a life. The poet Jennifer Moxley describes her first visit to the Waldrops' home:

---

[12] Knowles, *Memoir*, p.112.
[13] Wayne Franklin, *The Norton Anthology of American Literature, Vol. A*, p.193.
[14] Waldrop, *Ceci*, p.88.
[15] Keith Waldrop, *Ceci n'est pas Keith* (Providence, RI: Burning Deck, 2002) p.51.
[16] Waldrop, 'The Ground is the Only Figure,' p.224.

> Past the nineteen-fifties era shops lining Wayland Square we drove, until we came upon the long, straight, and peaceful Elmgrove Avenue, which though naked of elms for many years yet boasted other fine trees and many neatly manicured houses [...] The house awaiting us was dim and brooding, painted the darkest of browns, with a forest green trim, as if it were dressed to be camouflaged behind the masculine holly standing guard out front. No curtain was drawn, no sound nor light emanated from within, all was totally quiet. There was a strange metal box sitting by the door and an outdoor thermometer reading 38 degrees nailed into a shingle.[17]

Books are everywhere, along with collages, and seats, and curtains, and shadow. In the basement, the Heidelberg press, other letter presses, boxes of type, and books, the home of Burning Deck Press. As Gaston Bachelard once put it in *The Poetics of Space*, 'all really inhabited space bears the essence of the notion of home.'[18]

---

[17] Jennifer Moxley, 'A Personal Reminiscence Chronicling the First Documented Case of "The Waldrop Effect,"' *How2*, Vol. 1, No. 8 (Fall 2002), http://www.asu.edu/ pipercwcenter/how2journal/archive/online_archive/v1_8_2002/current/readings/moxley.htm, accessed 24 July 2012.

[18] Gaston Bachelard, *The Poetics of Space* (Boston, MA: Beacon Press, 1994) p.5.

Burning Deck

In 2011 Burning Deck celebrated its 50th anniversary. This is a remarkable achievement, not least for the financial longevity of a small poetry press, run from the Waldrops' own home, which operates on a non-commercial business model and which, by their own admission, tries 'to provide a forum for works of unconventional, innovative character, which commercial publishers are increasingly reluctant to take chances on.'[1] Burning Deck has published some of the most important experimental writers of the late twentieth and early twenty-first centuries. As Michael Palmer paid tribute in 1991, 'It occurs to me that without Burning Deck and a very few others, we experimental poets would, simply, not exist.'[2] Waldrop has described it as 'a small thing, it's very much in the margin, but it happens, it works [...] But you will never make money that way. That's clear. It's an alternate way of doing things.'[3] Today, Burning Deck is in a position to publish only four books per year—two by American poets and two volumes in translation of either French or German poetry—but its influence over the shape and texture of American poetic experiment is still considerable. Michael Tod Egerton, with a particular focus on the American context of the press, has remarked that 'thanks to the seemingly tireless efforts of the press' proprietors, Keith and Rosmarie Waldrop, (along with Alison Bundy, more recently) for nearly half a century Burning Deck has been a home to some of the most intelligent, formally engaged, innovative, and just straight-up exciting poetry being written in this country.' And Burning Deck, Egerton continues, 'has been a home to many varieties of language-centered, critical, and exploratory poetries over the years, making an indelible mark on American experimental poetry and its sustained conversation with its French and German analogs. We have much to thank the Waldrops for as the press approaches its fiftieth anniversary, and much cause to hope Burning Deck continues its work for many years to come.'[4] Likewise, Susan Smith Nash has written how

---

[1] Joseph Barbato, 'On the Edge with Burning Deck', *Publisher's Weekly* Vol. 237, No.33 (1990) p.40.
[2] Michael Palmer, quoted in Steve Evans, 'Rosmarie Waldrop.'
[3] Jared Demick, 'An Interview with Keith and Rosmarie Waldrop,' *The Jivin' Ladybug*, http://mysite.verizon.net/vze8911e/jivinladybug/id53.html, accessed 10 July 2011.
[4] Michael Tod Egerton, 'This Half-Life Explicated by Touch: On Two Recent Books by Burning Deck Press', *Jacket*, 40 (Late 2010), http://jacketmagazine.com/40/edgerton-on-the-burning-deck.shtml, accessed 5 July 2012.

'Burning Deck is one of those amazing independent publishers that seems to be in an eternal state of creation and recreation. What they publish consistently seems fresh, new, and noteworthy.'[5]

Burning Deck's origins were as a poetry magazine. Originally intended as a 'quinterly', *Burning Deck* magazine actually appeared only four times in five years. Despite its irregularity, though, two features of this start-up magazine were to have, albeit very different, lasting consequences, particularly in terms of Waldrop's own development as a poet. The first was *Burning Deck*'s method of production. Purchasing an old Chandler and Price letterpress for $100 from a print shop going out of business, the Waldrops typeset and printed the magazine by hand. This is a slow and laborious mode of production and often there are false starts and mistakes. The Waldrops maintained this process of production long after *Burning Deck* magazine had given way to Burning Deck press and long after it was strictly necessary, stopping letterpress production only in 1985 once developments in automated bookbinding meant it was much more cost effective to print full books offset. But the processes of typesetting, printing and binding were also as much about the experience of language as material—as substance, surface, object— as it was about economic realities. As Waldrop comments, 'I like setting type and printing in spite of its drudgery [...] I love holding in my hands a book I have made—such a tangible counterpart to reading and writing. Setting type by hand is so slow it seemed the invention of close reading.'[6] It also taught Waldrop the importance of concision in poetry: in letterpress, every letter counts.

Commenting at a forum on gender and editing in 1994, Waldrop remarked:

> In a tangible way, it is printing, even more than editing, that has affected my own writing. Printing letterpress (especially setting poems by hand, as we did in the beginning) is so slow a process that I became extremely aware of any unnecessary 'fat'. It has helped make my poems leaner.

Glenn Storhaug, the editor and publisher of Five Seasons Press, puts it in the following terms:

---

[5] Susan Smith Nash, '*Two Score and More*', *Review of Contemporary Fiction* (Summer 2003), p.141.
[6] Waldrop, *Ceci*, p.77.

> The letterpress hand compositor not only feels the weight of each word—and the weight of the surrounding space—in his stick, he also has to wrestle with all the different margins as he locks up his four or eight pages in the chase … In a page containing a poem set to wide measure but with many short lines, the spaces will demand more attention, and weigh more, than the type.[7]

The materiality of the page, the shape and pacing of type, white space, are more than the sum of their parts. As Storhaug continues:

> The successful page releases the text to meet the reader. Generous margins (with no unnecessary folios or other clutter) and ample leading create space and light against which the words stand like branches against the sky or images in stained glass: light shines *through* rather than *on to* the poem so each word is given a three-dimensional presence. Sharp printing (ideally letterpress) of a carefully chosen face at least 12 points in size—with careful word spacing acting as punctuation where the poem demands it—is of course essential for the achievement of this effect. Silence and speech, as light and shade, work in measure on the page, the poem breathes, the poet sings in the reader's head.[8]

Or as Bernard Noël has it, 'white space is silent, but not mute, and it produces a resonance whose vibrations let us feel the limits of language—or its song at the edge of disappearance—or perhaps the trajectory of the verbal event,'[9] even as, in Olson's phrase, it is also the case that, inevitably, 'ONE PERCEPTION MUST IMMEDIATELY AND DIRECTLY LEAD TO A FURTHER PERCEPTION.'[10]

The other significant feature of the original magazine that has continued to cast influence over both Burning Deck's catalogue and Waldrop's own poetry is its eclecticism. As the Waldrops, with neat sidestep of the somewhat critically overstated 'anthology wars' between Donald Hall and Donald Allen, wrote in the preface to *A Century in Two Decades*, their anthology celebrating the first 20 years of Burning Deck:

---

[7] Glenn Storhaug, 'On Printing Aloud', http://www.fiveseasonspress.com/printingaloud.pdf, accessed 12 October 2011.
[8] ibid.
[9] Bernard Noël, *Je te continue ma lecture*, p.136; quoted in *Lavish Absence*, p.97.
[10] Olson, 'Projective Verse,' *Selected Writings* (New York: New Directions, 1997) p.17.

> In 1961, poets were supposed to be in opposing camps, often inelegantly—and inaccurately—labelled 'academics' or 'beats'. The two most widely noted anthologies of the time, both representing the period 1945-1960, contain not a single poet in common.
> *Burning Deck* (the magazine) disregarded this split, printing and reviewing a spread of poets wide enough that on occasion an author would complain of being published in such unprogrammatic company.[11]

Even though limited resources have meant Burning Deck subsequently has had to narrow its non-partisan focus and concentrate, almost exclusively, on so-called 'innovative poetries', the promotion of eclecticism has always remained as a strongly inclusive principle behind editorial policy. As Rosmarie puts it, 'we have a definite preference for experimental work, but we're not tied to it.' And as Keith adds, 'we're not tied to any one experiment.'[12] But eclecticism as editorial policy is also politically loaded:

> Since being eclectic is not always taken for a virtue, we would note that our eclecticism—besides simply reflecting personal ranges of appreciation—is based on an inability to believe that the history of, for instance, poetry can possibly be clear before the poems are written. It is not denying the importance of 'movements', to insist that there is another importance in moving beside or apart from them. After all, there are many judgements, none of them the last.[13]

These last sentences are revealing. Just as Waldrop's life and poetry are marked by the 'between', so Burning Deck has never sat neatly within any of the available moulds of American poetics, experimental or otherwise. More than that, though, Burning Deck hasn't done so deliberately. There may well be strength in numbers but, after all, poetry is a world limited enough as it is and, anyway, it is not always possible to know from where the next surprise is likely to spring which is why it is called a surprise in the first place. No need to blinker unnecessarily and programme a sense of the proper. And besides, even

---

[11] Keith and Rosmarie Waldrop, 'Preface', *A Century in Two Decades: A Burning Deck Anthology, 1961-1981* (Providence, RI: Burning Deck, 1982) p.9.
[12] Joseph Barbato, 'On the Edge with Burning Deck,' *Publisher's Weekly*, 17 August 1990, p.40.
[13] Keith and Rosmarie Waldrop, *op. cit.*, p.11.

as preferences are part and parcel of living, all hands are sufficiently discrete to accommodate variety and a body, always, wants more than one thing. Thus the range of the poets included in Burning Deck magazine's four issues: Robert Creeley, Robert Duncan, Donald Finkel, Kathleen Fraser, Barbara Guest, Heath-Stubbs, LeRoi Jones (later, Amiri Baraka), Robert Kelly, X.J. Kennedy, Denise Levertov, Philip Levine, W.S. Merwin, Christopher Middleton, Natalie Robins, Louis Zukofsky.

After *Burning Deck* magazine came to an end in 1965, the Waldrops turned to publishing occasional chapbooks under the Burning Deck imprint. The first of these, in 1967, were a translation of Lorca's *Poem of the Gypsy Seguidilla*, printed in 'a small edition for friends' and with a cover and title page containing woodcuts by Keith, and Waldrop's own 24 paged *A Dark Octave* in an edition of 100 numbered copies, each bearing a two colour cover title page with a linoleum cut also by Keith. These were followed by Alan Sondheim's *An Ode (poems)* in 1968 and James Camp's *An Edit from the Emperor* in 1969. In 1970 Burning Deck published: Dorothy Donnelly's *Houses*, the first book of John Heath-Stubbs' *Artorius*, Peyton Houston's *For the Remarkable Animals*, X.J. Kennedy's *Bulsh*, Christopher Middleton's *The Fossil Fish*, Carl Morse's *Dive*, Terry Stokes' concisely titled *The Night Ed Sullivan Slapped One of the Kessler Twins Right on the Ass in the Middle of His Show & Their Song & Dance*, two by Waldrop: *The Relaxed Abalone; or, What-You-May-Find* in an edition of 150 numbered copies and *Camp Printing*, 500 copies offset from letterpress and 'containing collage transformations of poems by James Camp,' along with Rosmarie and Keith's collaborative collection of visual poems, *Letters*, printed in an edition of 500 numbered copies and signed on the cover by both authors.

When the National Endowment for the Arts began to provide financial assistance to independent publishing in 1973 Burning Deck was able to move into the publication of full-length books 'and broaden the program to include some fiction and, a little later, translations.'[14] The first of these publications was Anthony Barnett's long but linguistically sparing *Poem about Music*, followed by Keith Waldrop's *The Garden of Effort*, printed in an edition of 1000 copies in 1975 and with its apt epigraph from Saint Theresa advising that 'there are many ways of being

---

[14] Demick, 'Interview with Keith and Rosmarie Waldrop.'

in a place.'[15]

The critical importance of such institutions as the National Endowment for the Arts, the Goethe House, or the Cultural Services of the French Embassy to the development of Burning Deck (as well as other small presses, both then and now) cannot be overestimated. As one of the first policy statements of the National Endowment for the Arts put it in 1965:

> In a society which has always been marked by that special disorder which comes of vast spaces, a highly diversified people, great natural and technical resources, and a rapid tempo of historical change, the arts are here of utmost importance—not only as a moral force, but as a celebration of the American experience which encourages, clarifies and points to the next direction in our struggle to achieve the promise of our democracy.[16]

Indeed, as Donna M. Binkiewicz illustratively summarises, two distinct principles motivated the formation of American national arts policy and the foundation of the National Endowment for the Arts in 1965:

> One focused on domestic policy and began as a reaction to 1950s cultural criticism that accused the United States of having become conformist, materialist, complacent, and aesthetically deplorable. In response to such reproaches American intellectuals and leaders decided to enlist the arts as a means of social uplift [...] The second rationale for arts policy extended beyond American domestic policy to include a larger international mission. Presidential papers and congressional records demonstrate that the Cold War proved an important impetus in arts policy development during the Kennedy, Johnson, and Nixon presidencies. American leaders endeavored to outshine the Soviets in cultural displays and by so doing entice developing nations away from the lures of communist culture.[17]

---

[15] Keith Waldrop, *The Garden of Effort* (Providence, RI: Burning Deck, 1975) p.4
[16] 'National Endowment for the Arts Annual Report: 1964-1965,' in *Papers of the Chairman, Roger Stevens*, Box 15-21, National Endowment for the Arts (NEA), Washington.
[17] Donna M. Binkiewicz, *Federalizing the Muse: United States Art Policy and the National Endowment for the Arts 1965-1980* (The University of North Carolina Press, 2004), pp.3-4.

In such a political environment, however, the type of literary practice the NEA might deem worthy of financial assistance tended to be predominantly traditional in look and scope. Needless to say, in order to determine what type of work best exemplifies and expresses American culture, there necessarily needs to be a divisive understanding of what constitutes American culture in the first place, of what's in and what's not. Thus it was only when arts policy began to diversify in the 1970s that entrepreneurial activities such as independent publishing found themselves included within the NEA's mandate. As Rosmarie explains, '[y]ou had to match the amount the NEA gave you, but you could match it in labour.'[18] Even if this is the case, however, the fact remains that a pot of pennies (the NEA's entire budget measured only $145 million in 2009) split in many directions cannot reach all pockets. And anyway, as William Osborne notes, 'America advocates supply-side economics, small government and free trade—all reflecting a belief that societies should minimize government expenditure and maximize deregulated, privatized global capitalism.'[19] It is difficult to see where the arts fit into such an economic model, and the so-called innovative arts in particular: small press poetry can rarely, if ever, underwrite itself.

Significantly, in 1984, Burning Deck merged with ANYART: Contemporary Arts Center, becoming the literature programme of that non-profit organisation. In 1990 Burning Deck expanded its list to include the annual volume of translated French poetry, *Série d'écriture* (although always edited by Waldrop, originally produced in mimeograph by Paul Green's English press, Spectacular Diseases, until Burning Deck took over the production from Issue 6) and, in 1994, the German translation series, *Dichten=*. To date, Burning Deck has published over 200 original full-length volumes. Selections from the majority of these have been compiled into two anthologies, *A Century in Two Decades* and *One Score More*. And as the Waldrops wrote in the preface to that second volume in 2002, 'materials are accumulating towards a third anthology.'[20]

Burning Deck's awards and recognitions are numerous and international: in November 1991 the Foundation Royaumont in

---

[18] Demick, *op. cit.*
[19] William Osborne, 'Marketplace of Ideas: But First, the Bill: A Personal Commentary on American and European Cultural Funding,' *ArtsJournal*, 18th February 2004, http://www.artsjournal.com/artswatch/20040218-11320.shtml, accessed 7th September 2010.
[20] Rosmarie and Keith Waldrop, *One Score More: The Second 20 Years of Burning Deck, 1981-2001* (Providence, RI: Burning Deck, 2002) p.10.

France hosted a weekend symposium on Burning Deck while the Centre International de Poésie in Marseille staged an exhibition on the small press. Peter Gizzi's American journal *O.blek* ran an issue devoted to the work of Burning Deck in 1991 while, in 1996, the Paris-based magazine, *Prétexte*, published a special issue of Burning Deck poets in French translation, including: Rae Armantrout, Tina Darragh, Michael Davidson, Larry Eigner, Michael Gizzi, Barbara Guest, Julie Kalendek, Harry Mathews, Claire Needell, Gale Nelson, Ray Ragosta, Cole Swensen, Keith Waldrop, and Craig Watson. The recipient of various national and international grants, Burning Deck has also been the focus of exhibitions staged by Intersection in San Francisco, the bookshop Woodland Pattern in Milwaukee, and Brown University library between March and April 2001. Most recently, Po Gallery in Providence, Rhode Island have staged an exhibition celebrating the 50th anniversary of Burning Deck.

Bottom Line Abacus

For a small press, Burning Deck's longevity is remarkable. In interview Keith Waldrop has lightheartedly put this permanence down to 'pigheadedness' but in many ways stubbornness is probably accurate enough.[1] With high costs, time-intensive labour and limited sales, small press publishing does not produce an economy of sustainable scale. In economic terms, the business of poetry is not so much a trade related to profit-led consumerism as it is by the more informal and non-monetary custom of local communities, social networks and gift economies. On this model, poetry is not a commodity. Rather, the production and distribution (giving) of poetry takes place within the context of non-monetary social networks, themselves organised by notions of kinship, mutual interest and status and which, crucially, are structured by the informally mandated proposition that '*the gift must always move.*'[2] In other words, in such communities, 'whatever [is] given is supposed to be given away not kept. Or, if it is kept, something of similar value should move in its stead.'[3] It is in this way that poetry not only enters the world of exchange but finds a readership and stays there. As Rosmarie Waldrop puts it in interview, '[w]ord of mouth is actually a powerful force. Word travels, our little books have traveled to places where we're astonished to find them. It's a small thing, it's very much in the margin of [the commercial market], but it happens, it works.'[4] (It is also interesting to note that it is for this reason that the Waldrops have continued to maintain Burning Deck, despite its small-scale, for half a century; as long as Burning Deck continues to exist, its back catalogue is protected from market place trends and remains in circulation in perpetuity. As Rosmarie Waldrop comments in interview, 'as soon as a press stops being active, the back catalog practically dies. We have a huge backlist [...] If we keep the press active we also keep the older books alive.')[5]

In the context of poetry publishing, particularly important here is the notion that it may well be that such gift economies are not simply the mainstay of present and future models of poetic production but also

---

[1] Demick, 'Interview with Keith and Rosmarie Waldrop.'
[2] Lewis Hyde, *The Gift: Creativity and the Artist in the Modern World* (London: Vintage, 2007) p.4.
[3] ibid.
[4] Demick, *op. cit.*
[5] ibid.

the grounds for its self-legitimation, which is to say, the very reason for these social networks to exist already in the first place. According to Charles Bernstein:

> These institutions continue, against all odds, to find value in the local, the particular, the partisan, the committed, the tiny, the peripheral, the unpopular, the eccentric, the difficult, the complex, the homely; and in the formation and reformation, dissolution and questioning, of imaginary or virtual or partial or unavowable communities and/or uncommunities.[6]

To put it another way, small press publishing, distribution, subscriptions, mailing and sales depend upon a community of readers: friends, colleagues, organisations, institutions, patrons. It is made up of a network of connections, of like-minded people and people who would like to be like-minded. Under such conditions, as Nicholas Michael Ravnikar notes, 'small press economics doesn't need to give the caveat common to other market analysis. With small presses, ceteris is never paribus.'[7] Yet if this is the case, understanding the value of what is being given or exchanged becomes crucially important, particularly when that poetic gift depends upon the financial input of grants funding and patronage in order to take place at all. Indeed, as Christopher Beach has commented:

> In historical terms, the United States has a greater abundance of poets and of poetry than ever before. It also has a healthy supply of presses and journals of various kinds to publish that poetry. The question is, are there enough readers of poetry to sustain or justify such an output, in either economic or cultural terms?[8]

It is a difficult question and one which the frequent argument that the value of such poetry can only be quantified through qualitative measurement does little to nullify or obviate.

---

[6] Charles Bernstein, 'Provisional Institutions: Alternative Presses and Poetic Innovation', *My Way: Speeches and Poems* (Chicago: The University of Chicago Press, 1999) p.154.
[7] Nicholas Michael Ravnikar, 'Pre-Calculus for Small Press Publishers', *Woodland Pattern*, http://woodlandpattern.blogspot.com/2010/03/pre-calculus-for-small-press-publishers.html, accessed 19th May 2011.
[8] Christopher Beach, *Poetic Culture: Contemporary American Poetry Between Community and Institution* (Evanston, IL: Northwestern University Press, 1999) p.21.

Bottom Line Abacus 57

As Chris Hamilton-Emery, Director of Salt Publishing, emphasises, 'The market for selling poetry is, in relation to the total book trade, an extremely small one, and it is complex, fragmented, well-managed and highly competitive. Because of this, it is notoriously difficult to coordinate a sustainable economic model for contemporary writing.'[9] Like most independent literary presses, Burning Deck's non-commercial business model has the advantage of largely sidestepping bottom line barometers, enabling them to publish 'experimental' works that may not generate any kind of financial return, or break even, but it also affords no lasting security.[10] Besides, as Rosmarie Waldrop has commented in interview, in a typical print run of 1,000 copies, a significant percentage of these are given away as review copies or as exchanges.

So it is that it is not always prudent to carry out a risk assessment on what we do for a living for fear that we will no longer do it. Indeed, as Rusty Morrison, co-editor of the independent press Omnidawn Publishing, comments: 'Poetry books are generally published in quantities of a thousand copies or less, and it is impossible for such runs to pay the expenses.'[11] Even despite Burning Deck's considerable cultural influence and esteemed reputation, the fact of the matter remains that Burning Deck's continued existence relies almost exclusively on public grants, subsidies, and private investment. To take just one example, here is the acknowledgements list of financial benefactors of Burning Deck from 1981-2001:

> the National Endowment for the Arts, RI State Council on the Arts, the Fund for Poetry, Taft Memorial Fund, the Cultural Services of the French Embassy, Pro Helvetia Foundation, Inter Nationes, and the following individuals: Craig Watson, Chris & Jeanne Longyear, Leonard Brink, Rachel Blau Duplessis, Harry Matthews, Eliot Weinberger, Kenneth Fain & Lisa Gim, Connie Coleman & Alan Powell, Christopher Middleton, Steve Evans, Patrick O'Shea, Shelby Matthews, Rena Rosenwasser, Roger Stoddard, Lawrence Fixel, Michael Gizzi, Romana Huk, Jay Scrivener, Karen Weiser.

---

[9] Chris Hamilton-Emery, *101 Ways to Make Poems Sell: The Salt Guide to Getting and Staying Published* (Cambridge: Salt Publishing, 2006) p.87.
[10] For a breakdown of the costs and profits/losses of small press publishing see, Charles Bernstein, 'Provisional Institutions,' pp. 148-152.
[11] Rusty Morrison, 'Introducing Small Press Distribution,' http://www.abebooks.com/docs/Community/Featured/spd-omnidawn.shtml, accessed 6th September 2010.

Most of these private benefactors are poets themselves. It is not surprising. To a large extent, poets tend to be the ones who finance poetry—those that do, generally, though not always, are those that buy, support, invest. And this is so for obvious reasons: where, for instance, the contemporary visual arts can function equally as investment plan product and modish backdrop to polite conversation, a book of poetry is a more private affair and economies of fashion have always been visual rather than written. Accordingly, the business of poetry offers little in the way of remuneration packages and relies more and more on poets being consumers first, driving and sustaining their own marketplace of circulation and exchange. Yet that also means, then, that, first and foremost, poetic ventures are the product of other economies because all money has to come from somewhere and, no matter how much certain persons might want it, there is no such thing as poetry for the sake of poetry just as no job title can read poet only. The 'donation' by Ruth Lilly of $100 million to the subsequently privatised and renamed Poetry Foundation in 2003 is a relatively recent case in point, particularly given that this money originates from the profits of the pharmaceutical trade. In addition to this, though, and as Chad Harbach has illustratively discussed, the need for an external income to fund the work of poets and small press publishers also accounts for the increasing incorporation of the poet within the higher education system, whereby their livelihood and ability to write and publish poetry is not simply sustained but is made possible by teaching. As Harbach puts it:

> The poet earns money as a teacher; and, at a higher level of professional accomplishment, from grants and prizes; and, at an even higher level, from appearance fees at other colleges. She does not, as a rule, earn money by publishing books of poems—it has become almost inconceivable that anyone outside a university library will read them. The consequences of this economic arrangement for the quality of American poetry have been often bemoaned (poems are insular, arcane, gratuitously allusive, etc.), if poorly understood. Of more interest here is the economic arrangement proper.[12]

On this model, then, the single most important currency in poetry is not so much money as the time money can buy. Thus the primary

---

[12] Chad Harbach, 'MFA vs. NYC', *Slate Magazine*, http://www.slate.com/id/2275733/pagenum/all/, accessed 19 May 2011.

importance of grants, awards, patronage, gifts, underwriting, specifically in terms of the ways in which each enables this work to be done in the first place but also, crucially, in terms of how any award guarantees access to this work, at least for a certain amount of time (quantity of time obviously depends upon quantity of award relative to organisational size; as with most things, here number and longevity are directly equivalent).

Yet even time supported cannot an entire empire sustain and the financial foundations of a small poetry press are shaky at best. As Waldrop noted in 1996, over the course of a year, for the whole of the United States, the NEA spent:

> less than the *city* of Paris;
> what the Pentagon spends in 5 hours 26 minutes and 12 seconds;
> what costs each taxpayer $.64, i.e., 2 postage stamps.[13]

Even if the cost of typesetting, proofreading, paper, and printing, together with associated costs such as rent, utilities and equipment, are counter-balanced by sales, one of the biggest problems facing the sustainability of the small press is the cost of distribution, such that Charles Bernstein could note in 1999 how 'Small Press Distribution is the most important source for alternative press titles published in the United States.'[14] Like other independent distributors, such as the Independent Publishers Group in the US or Inpress Books in the UK, Small Press Distribution (SPD) serves over 400 independent presses, the majority of which have no other source of distribution. As SPD's own website defines the organisation's aims and scope:

> SPD allows essential but under-represented literary communities to participate fully in the marketplace and in the culture at large through book distribution, information services, and public advocacy programs. SPD nurtures an environment in which the literary arts are valued and sustained.[15]

Yet even SPD, which on average needs to take around 55% of a title's sales price, relies almost exclusively on private patronage and government grants to stay afloat. Indeed, as both Waldrop and

---

[13] Waldrop, 'The Ground is the Only Figure,' p.255.
[14] Bernstein, 'Provisional Institutions', p.152.
[15] 'About SPD,' http://www.spdbooks.org/pages/about/default.aspx, accessed 6 September 2010.

Bernstein have each separately noted, small press poetry publishing is an example of what 'George Bataille has called general economy, an economy of loss rather than accumulation. Poetry is a negative—or let's just say poetic—economy.'[16]

And thus Waldrop's argument in her important essay 'Alarms and Excursions' detailing how the effort of writing and publishing is far in excess of any material or measurable reward. Small press publishing, she maintains, exists somewhere between the demands of free markets and an economy of waste. On the one hand, 'it is obvious that the energy that goes into writing a poem is enormous and totally out of proportion to any gain it might bring [...] even if we include non-monetary gains like reputation, approbation of a group etc.' On the other hand:

> As far as publisher or bookseller being enriched, this holds for some books, but I doubt it ever holds for poetry, and obviously not for the small presses and their distributors which have no hope of even breaking even and must rely on grants or patronage. And I would like to see the bookseller who gets rich by stocking small press poetry. In other words, the whole small press world, rather than getting rich at the poets' expense, is like the poets, engaged in wasting energy, time, money; wasting it beautifully.[17]

Of course, not every thing is merchandise to be traded or even used but no matter how one looks at it a book costs and a specialist book with a small readership costs even more, and a finely made specialist book with a small readership costs even more again. For Waldrop, the small press poetry publisher at best occupies a somewhat paradoxical social position—while their labour is not so much motivated by the financial basis of the marketplace they are still actually engaged in the business of producing a saleable commodity. The crucial point is that small press poetry publishing operates with a business model whereby the cost of production outweighs all and any return. And thus it's one thing to be given a grant to begin but when each print run produces an overall net loss, it's quite another to continue. It is in this way that small press poetry publishing exceeds Marx's sense of a restricted economy (with its bottom line barometer of market value) and yields rather a so-called general economy or economy of (beautiful) waste that has eyes

---

[16] Bernstein, 'Provisional Institutions', p.150.
[17] Waldrop, 'Alarms and Excursions,' p.50.

only on the present. As Waldrop writes:

> The key word here is the *present*, not being constrained by any considerations of the future in which the work might be read, appreciated, sold [...] In contrast, if I am concerned with building a career I write as an investment rather than spending [...] My eye is on the market, maybe just on the approval of a group, in any case on the future. I voluntarily submit to the order of reality, to the laws which ensure the maintenance of life or of career.[18]

Steve McCaffery applies and develops these economic distinctions to the cultural consequence of poetry in general, especially in terms of the privileged status meaning occupies over method in poetry. Content, McCaffery argues, is always and again privileged over form (such that the experience of reading a poem is parallel to asking *but what does it mean?*) in a restrictive economy. In a general economy, on the other hand, form is privileged over content; the medium is the message:

> Restricted economy, which is the economy of Capital, Reason, Philosophy, and History, will always strive to govern writing, to force its appearance through an order of constraints. The general economy would forfeit this government, conserve nothing, and, while not prohibiting meaning's appearance, would only sanction its profitless emergence in general expenditure: hence, it would be entirely indifferent to results and concerned only with self-dispersal. A general economy can never be countervaluational nor offer an alternative 'value' to Value, for it is precisely the operation of value that it explicitly disavows.[19]

At issue here is the difficult and often highly contradictory notion of poetic value. In financial terms, there is little or no 'gain' from poetry. The economy of poetry is an economy of loss rather than growth. In relation to this, for Charles Bernstein the value of poetry is not to be determined by its economic role but rather by a particular understanding of its cultural function:

---

[18] Waldrop, 'Alarms and Excursions', p.51.
[19] Steve McCaffery, *North of Intention: Critical Writings, 1973-1986* (Toronto: Nightwood Editions, 1986) p.202.

Poetry's social function is to imagine how language works within its culture, while pursuing a critique of the culture; this suggests that poetry can be a countermeasure to the reinforcement of cultural values at the heart of both popular entertainment and consumer politics. At the same time, poetry's aesthetic function is to refuse even this 'value' in the pursuit of what Louis Zukofsky calls the pleasures of sight, sound, and intellect.[20]

Such notions of non-monetary value no doubt also go some way to explaining the cultural marginalisation, in relative terms, of poetry: in a sale or return culture there is little room for a literary form which doesn't simply critique that culture but which even devalues the very terms of its own 'value' in favour of complex categories such as aesthetics which, arguably, are even more abstract than money. This is Bernstein again:

> The very distance that separates poetry from the dominant forms of the macro economy of accumulation give poetry a social, political, and aesthetic power, because—at least potentially—poetry's realizations of, and reflection on, its 'host' culture are not only trenchant but otherwise unobtainable. A culture that despises its artists may need them even more than one that embraces them.[21]

As Bernstein continues:

> Since the mass scale of journalism and movies and pop music undermine the criteria of evaluation in our culture, it's important to emphasize that a singular value of poetry is the freedom, complexity, and depth that derives from its small scale, the fact that it has few readers, that it is difficult to access, that it's not a mass art form.[22]

In other words, one of the principal values of poetry—its unique selling point, if you will—is that it is read by few people. There is a fairly familiar theoretical argument here which, by and large, still tends to hold sway in the large majority of contemporary avant-garde circles; it is an argument that stretches back at least to Romanticism but which

---

[20] Eric Denut, 'Interview with Charles Bernstein,' *The Argotist Online*, http://www.argotistonline.co.uk/Bernstein%20interview.htm, accessed 20 May 2011.
[21] ibid.
[22] ibid.

arguably receives most of its contemporary force from current readings of, among others, Theodor Adorno, Walter Benjamin, Philippe Lacoue-Labarthe and Jean-Luc Nancy.[23] As Bernstein continues elsewhere, 'the power of our alternative institutions of poetry is their commitment to scales that allow for the flourishing of the artform, not the maximizing of the audience.'[24]

For Bernstein and Waldrop, as well as small press publishing more generally, the aim is for a literary work to be perceived as something rather more than a 'mere counter of exchange.'[25] Implicit within Bernstein's critique of the commercial publishing industry is what he perceives to be the profit-driven influence of its marketing spend where marketing campaigns are directed less, if at all, towards introducing readers to work that is innovative, unfamiliar and new but rather towards the 'manufacturing [of] renown.'[26] In commercial publishing, benchmarking is key whereas in small press publishing difference is everything: commercial publishing seeks classification because such categories provide both marketing strategies and sales potential (*if you like this, you'll love this*); small press publishing, on the other hand, establishes value by privileging aesthetic exclusivity. *Technē*, for instance, is a quality inseparably linked to that *singular* poet and which can be neither fully reproduced nor bought wholesale. Put another way, commercial publishing is contractual; small press publishing is social.

Waldrop does not go quite as far as this in 'Alarms and Excursions', partly perhaps because her concerns in that essay are frequently more practical than aesthetic, and partly because, as she comments, 'for all our anarchic intensity, sooner or later we want our mss. published. We want to be both reckless *and* read.'[27] Yet McCaffery's point about general expenditure is a useful one, particularly in terms of its conviction of the importance of the social function of poetry to extract words from reference and to draw 'attention to the word as object,' as something a little more than a 'mere counter of exchange.'[28]

For all that critical function, though, it is worth repeating that there is no escaping the bottom line: it still costs to produce poetry and all

---

[23] For more on this, see my 'The Poetics of Emergency', *Jacket*, Vol. 32 (April, 2007), http://jacketmagazine.com/32/p-duffy.shtml.
[24] Bernstein, 'Provisional Institutions,' p.153.
[25] Waldrop, 'Alarms and Excursions,' p.60.
[26] Bernstein, *op. cit.*, 154.
[27] Waldrop, 'Alarms and Excursions,' p.51.
[28] ibid, p.60.

invoices, no matter how well filed, need paying at some point. Besides, not even privilege exclusively exists in a vacuum just as even the most radical of enterprises needs some form of nourishment and all food costs money somewhere along the way. So it is that someone needs to foot the bill and shortfalls bridged over. And thus the vital importance of supportive federal arts policy, and in particular such organisations as the National Endowment for the Arts with its—albeit occasional and lottery based—grants system for the promotion of aesthetic excellence and public accessibility of the arts in general.

In this context, then, and leaving aside the complicated matter of whether or not the arts should be publicly funded (although quite clearly they should be; let there be no more said about it) the more pressing issue becomes one of actively aiming to influence public arts policy. This is particularly the case in terms of shaping the principle criteria used for deciding what and why and who gets funded, as well as the methods by which any returns on that funding are underwritten, measured and judged. As it stands, impact continues to be measured by the bottom line abacus whereas, as Charles Bernstein suggests, 'the political power of poetry is not measured in numbers; it instructs us to count differently.'[29] Indeed, it is for this reason that Goethe House has ceased regular funding of Burning Deck's landmark and internationally renowned *Dichten=* series. As Waldrop explains:

> Even the Goethe House is now mostly turning us down. This began the moment they started requiring a sales report of the publications they had supported. Obviously, they were not impressed with the sales. I told them this doesn't mean that they are sitting in a warehouse. They go in other ways: exchanges, review books, especially a lot of exchanges. But this doesn't impress them it seems.[30]

Precisely which alternative methods of counting it would be more advisable to adopt, of course, remains somewhat uncertain. And in spite of everything, as Waldrop comments, 'there remains the huge doubt, the nagging suspicion of a quantitative threshold.'[31] Whatever the measure, though, the fact remains that the worlds of so-called

---

[29] Charles Bernstein, 'Comedy and the Poetics of Political Form,' *The Politics of Poetic Form*, p.242.
[30] Demick, 'Interview with Keith and Rosmarie Waldrop Interview.'
[31] Waldrop, 'Alarms and Excursions,' p.61.

innovative poetry and small press publishing each require financial assistance from one source or another. Besides, everything has to start from somewhere and when the banks fail it's always good to have a book or two to read, particularly ones which point to other futures by putting things together just that little bit differently. And even though 'poetry, like philosophy, leaves everything as it is [...] when your government consistently lies through its teeth, it just may be very important to pay attention to words in the way poetry does.'[32]

---

[32] Matthew Cooperman, 'Between Tongues: An Interview with Rosmarie Waldrop,' *Conjunctions* (2005), http://www.conjunctions.com/webcon/cooperman.htm, accessed 7th September 2010.

Exploring and Maintaining

In essay and interview Waldrop has also referred to a passage in Ernest Fenellosa's *Notes on the Chinese Written Character* which applies equally well to her own practice of poetics:

> A true noun, an isolated thing, does not exist in nature. Things are only terminal points, or rather the meeting points, of actions, cross-sections cut through actions, snap-shots. Neither can a pure verb, an abstract motion, be possible in nature […] thing and action cannot be separated.[1]

For Waldrop the interest of this passage lies in the way Fenellosa's question of how snap-shots, meeting points glimpsed on the bluff, might be collected, how different facts might be held in relation without their difference being collapsed into the same, raises the essential question of poetry and, by extension, that of living. The world is not discrete but continuous and the single poem opens, necessarily, into sequence, just as any totality of parts is composite and builds slowly and by tangents.

In many ways, the poetic sequence is an exemplary form for Waldrop, both figure and ground. It enables an extended project, commentary, or exposition without making universal gestures. As with, for example, Walter Benjamin's valorisation of the leaflet, brochure, newspaper article, placard and other ephemera, the episodic quality of the sequence enables disjuncture to become a central part of both the poem's form and content.[2] The early collection, *The Road is Everywhere or, Stop This Body* is a case in point. Incorporating the permeability of the outside world with traffic signs, traffic noise, streetlights, movement, and clatter, the sequence flows and fragments in equal measure, full of the irregularities and inconsistencies of material life, such as a still photograph of a traffic sign meant, at least partially, to represent the flow of constant moving traffic. Life is registered concretely, like cracks in the pavement, like mortar.

---

[1] Robert van Hallberg, 'Olson, Whitehead, and the Objectivists,' *Boundary 2*, Vol. 2, Nos.1-2 (1973-1974) p.109. Waldrop also refers to this quotation in her essay 'Charles Olson: Process and Relationship,' *Dissonance*, pp.58-80, and again in interview with Christine Hume, *12x12*, p.78.
[2] See Walter Benjamin, *One Way Street and Other Writings*, trans. J.A. Underwood (London: Penguin, 2009).

The American poet, Forrest Gander, has written how, 'in his own time, Giovanni Battista Vico argued against clear, distinct, Cartesian ideas, emphasizing instead practical wisdom and ingenium, the power of connecting separate and diverse elements.'[3]

In many ways, it is this path also which interests Waldrop.

'All I am saying,' Waldrop writes in the essay 'Thinking of Follows,' 'is on the surface, which is all we can work on. I like the image in *Don Quixote* that compares translation to working on a tapestry: you sit behind it, with a mess of threads and a pattern for each color, but have no idea of the image that will appear on the other side.' 'This,' Waldrop adds, 'holds for writing as well. We work on technical aspects, on the craft' and this craft correlates to the question of how to connect the separate and diverse while simultaneously allowing them to remain separate and diverse.[4] It is a question, in other words, of how to weave different parts together without smoothing over those differences. As Lyn Hejinian puts it:

> the very incapacity of language to match the world allows it to do service as a medium of differentiation. The undifferentiated is one mass, the differentiated is multiple. The (unimaginable) complete text, the text that contains everything, would be in fact a closed text. It would be insufferable.[5]

In a manner similar to Language poetry's—a group with which Waldrop has always been close although never directly affiliated—mistrust of narrativity, the ordering or the closure of the field of experience is what Waldrop's poetic seeks to resist. Waldrop equates this process to the non-representational language of music, particularly rhythm. As Barrett Warren outlined it in his essay, 'Nonnarrative and the Construction of History,' 'nonnarratives are forms of discursive presentation in which both linear and contextual syntax exist but where univocal motivation, retrospective closure, and transcendent perspective are suspended, deferred, or do not exist.'[6] Even if a field of reference emerges, Warren

---

[3] Forrest Gander, 'Nymph Stick Insect: Observations on Poetry, Science, Creation,' *A Faithful Existence: Reading, Memory, Transcendence* (Denver, CO: Counterpoint Press, 2005), p.14.
[4] Waldrop, 'Thinking of Follows,' p.208.
[5] Lyn Hejinian, 'The Rejection of Closure,' p.56.
[6] Barrett Warren, 'Nonnarrative and the Construction of History,' in Jerry Heron, Dorothy Hudson, Ross Pudaloff, and Robert Strozier (eds.), *The Ends of Theory* (Detroit, MI: Wayne State University, 1996) p.210.

continues, the effects of those referents are fundamentally dependent on the gaps and discontinuities through which they emerge.

Although it is arguable Waldrop learnt more about non-narrative from the example of Edmond Jabès than she did from Language poetry, in the context of this wider aesthetic, for Waldrop the primary and most vital element of a poem is rhythm. Rhythm, Waldrop comments, is that 'elusive quality without which there is no poem, without which the most interesting words remain mere words on paper, remain at best verse [...] Rhythm, I mean, not meter. It is difficult to talk about, impossible to pin down. It is the truly physical essence of the poem, determined by the rhythms of my body, my breath, my pulse. But it is also the alternation of sense and absence, sound and silence. It articulates the between, the difference in repetition.'[7] It is a site of equivocation, the 'double vision' of paradox which challenges each and any closed system.[8]

For Michael Palmer, a poem is 'a site of passages, full of noise and its silence [...] a space or region of paradox, contradiction and polysemy, a space, one is tempted to say, of poetry where the words we hear are both the same and different, recognizable and foreign, constructed in fact like language itself on the place of identity and difference.'[9]

According to the 17th century Jesuit priest, mathematician and physicist Francesco Maria Grimaldi, diffraction is the bending of waves around obstacles and the spreading out of waves past small openings. The effects of diffraction are most definite where the wavelength is of a similar size to the diffracting object. Small particles in the air can cause a bright ring to be visible around a bright light source such as the sun or a halogen lamp. The word 'diffraction' comes from the Latin *diffringere*, meaning 'to break into pieces'.

Thus, for Waldrop:

> discontinuity seems the natural state. It's how I see the world. We come to know anything that has any complexity by glimpses. So it is best to have as many different glimpses from as many different perspectives as possible, rather than trying to develop a linear argument where one follows from another.[10]

---

[7] Waldrop, 'Thinking of Follows,' p.213.
[8] Waldrop, 'Mirrors and Paradoxes,' *Dissonance*, p.81.
[9] Michael Palmer, 'Active Boundaries: Poetry at the Periphery' in *Active Boundaries: Selected Essays and Talks* (New York: New Directions, 2008) pp.208-9.
[10] 'Retallack, 'A Conversation,' p. 361.

Exploring and Maintaining

'I hope,' Waldrop writes, 'that the glimpses [...] amount to more than their sum, that they gain in intensity from allowing interruption, allowing possibility to enter.'[11] Or as Waldrop puts it in the aptly titled, 'Velocity but no location':

> There is a pleasure in composition, in grasping the connection of the one and the many. The way we gradually discover how the dancer's movements are anchored in, and anchor, the axis she spins around, the way the backbone is held up by the muscles acting in concert or our sense of self by the mirror. Without it we are forced into constant activity to make up for the lacking image.[12]

Or as Waldrop puts it in relation to Jabès in a description which applies equally well to her own work, 'shifting voices and constant breaks of mode let silence have its share and allow for a fuller meditative field than possible in linear narrative or analysis.'[13]

> Energy, matter. It exists, but it becomes 'world' only in the book, in language [...] Matter becomes the matter of words, which creates structure, makes legible, interprets, against a ground of unreadable silence.[14]

In her doctoral dissertation, defended at the University of Michigan in 1965 and published in 1967 as *Against Language?*, Waldrop puts this idea in the following terms: 'If language is an instrument of cognition, the act of writing a poem becomes an act of exploration, of knowledge.'[15] Or as Pound wrote in 1915: 'The essential thing about a poet is that he builds us his world.'[16] Waldrop frequently holds that poetry is not to be understood as a metaphor for the world; she is not trying to claim that the poem is analogous to the world's formation. Rather, the point

---

[11] Waldrop, *Lavish Absence*, p.19.
[12] Rosmarie Waldrop, 'Velocity but no location,' *Salt Magazine*, Issue 2 (April 2008), http://www.saltpublishing.com/saltmagazine/issues/02/text/Waldrop_Rosmarie.htm, accessed 05 July 2012. Reprinted in the chapbook, *Velocity But No Location* (San Francisco: Sardines Press, 2011).
[13] Waldrop, *Lavish Absence*, p.2.
[14] ibid, pp.1-2.
[15] Rosmarie Waldrop, *Against Language? 'dissatisfaction with language' as theme and as impulse towards experiments in twentieth century poetry* (The Hague: Mouton, 1971), p.11.
[16] Ezra Pound, *Selected Prose, 1909-1965*, ed. William Cookson (New York: New Directions, 1975) p.7.

is that, throughout the various trajectories of Waldrop's writing, poetry is an actual process of making; poetry functions as the very means through which the world becomes form, matter; and it does so, largely, in what it shows is unsaid.

Edmond Jabès: 'We know of silence only what words can tell us.'[17]

Maurice Blanchot: 'to write is to make oneself the echo of what cannot cease speaking—and since it cannot, in order to become its echo I have, in a way, to silence it. This silence has its source in the effacement toward which the writer is drawn.'[18] It is for this reason that the body can, on occasion, be known to sing just as it is also the reason why a body can be known to stand in a basement pressing letters until a book is made for reasons other than money. Language, Waldrop suggests, 'is created by man and at the same time creates him.'[19] This balance between life and language is precarious. It has collage at its root.

---

[17] Edmond Jabès, *A Foreigner Carrying in the Crook of his Arm a Tiny Book*, trans. Rosmarie Waldrop (Middletown, CT: Wesleyan University Press, 1993) p.45.
[18] Blanchot, *The Space of Literature*, p.27.
[19] Waldrop, *Lavish Absence*, p.1.

Collage

In a manner similar to the epic proportions of assemblage practiced by Walter Benjamin for his *Pasagen-Werken*, Waldrop's writing is grounded 'on philosophical intuitions sparked by cognitive experiences reaching as far back as childhood. These "develop" only in the sense that a photographic plate develops: time deepens definition and contrast, but the imprint of the image has been there from the start.'[1] In Waldrop ideas crystallise over time and, often, through reading. A passage read will spark a thought, a response, a phrase, a memory, a quotation, and somewhere between it all another text slowly begins to find form. 'The method of collage goes a long way to embodying the way I feel I am in the world. There is an immensity of data around us, and to choose the ones that are relevant and to connect them is my sense of life also.'[2]

In relation to this, Fiona McMahon terms Waldrop's poetry 'field verse' because 'it ties poetry to the materials of the writer, ranging from varieties of the typeface and characters to the bibliographical references and iconic documents.'[3] It is a life of the mind and the body and the book intertwined; it is a slow coming to, a personal dialectic of emergence, submergence, re-emergence, messianic, almost, redemptive. It is, Waldrop notes, a sense of writing 'as dialog with a whole web of previous and concurrent texts, with tradition, with the culture and language we breathe and move in and that conditions us even while we help to construct it.'[4]

Elsewhere Waldrop develops this sense of collage and links it to the apperception of the infinite, the ineffable: 'We can approach the infinite,' Waldrop writes, 'only through fragments.'[5] A world of fragments, but not necessarily a fragmentary world. Life stretches beyond itself, beyond what it has been possible to write, into the spaces of silence, the sites of turning. Fragments recur and alter, 'blend and clash' in Roland Barthes' famous phrase, and are constitutive matter. It is, quite literally, a material writing. In other words, it is a writing which both makes use of other 'material' and which mines material

---

[1] Susan Buck-Morris, *The Dialectics of Seeing: Walter Benjamin and the Arcades Project* (Cambridge, MA: MIT Press, 1991) p.7
[2] Joan Retallack, 'A Conversation,' p.370.
[3] Fiona McMahon, 'Rosmarie Waldrop: A Poetics of Contiguity', *Revue Francaise d'Etudes Americaines*, no. 103 (2005), p.65. [pp.64-78]
[4] Waldrop, 'Thinking of Follows,' p.207.
[5] Waldrop, 'Shall we escape analogy,' *Dissonance*, p.109.

experience for the coordinates necessary to plot a route through this material. As Walter Benjamin once remarked, collage is a progressive form because it 'interrupts the context into which it is inserted' and so 'counteracts illusion.'[6] As Waldrop puts it, 'there is no location, only comings and goings' and the wider work is made up of small, particular moments.[7] Collage says little but shows much, and what it shows more than anything else is difference.

Pierre Joris comments how painterly collage makes its discrete elements visible, whereas literary collage buries its borrowings, 'deriving its essential fracture from the seams that make clear the fact of heterogeneous elements being brought together.'[8] Charles Bernstein reinforces this sense of collage, writing how collage is 'the use of different textual elements without recourse to an overall unifying idea' and contrasting this notion of collage with the practice of montage which is defined as 'the use of contrasting images toward the goal of one unifying theme.'[9] Tracing the citational technique of collage back to the ancient patchwork practice of *cento*, Marko Juvan similarly outlines the ways in which collage 'defiantly undermines its own stylistic harmony and semantic coherence.'[10] According to Marjorie Perloff, 'collage has been the most important mode for representing a "reality" no longer quite believed in and therefore all the more challenging.'[11] Or, as the authors of the 1978 Group Mu manifesto put it: 'Each cited element breaks the continuity or the linearity of the discourse and leads necessarily to a double reading: that of the fragment perceived in relation to its text of origin; that of the same fragment as incorporated into a new whole, a different totality.'[12]

John Cage extends these ideas, suggesting that collage is exemplary because it correlates to a contemporary mode of living in the world. 'A great deal of our experiences,' Cage comments in interview, 'come from the large use of glass in our architecture, so that our experience is one

---

[6] Walter Benjamin, quoted in Buck-Morris, *The Dialectics*, p.67.
[7] Waldrop, 'Shall we escape analogy,' p.111.
[8] Pierre Joris, *A Nomad Poetics: Essays* (Middletown, CT: Wesleyan University Press, 2003) p.84.
[9] Charles Bernstein, quoted in Joris, *A Nomad Poetics*, p.87.
[10] Marko Juvan, *History and Poetics of Intertextuality*, trans. Timothy Pogačar (Purdue University Press, 2008) p.170.
[11] Marjorie Perloff, 'Collage and Poetry,' *Encyclopedia of Aesthetics*, ed. Michael Kelly (New York: Oxford University Press, 1998), Vol.1, p.385.
[12] Group *Mu*, 'Douze bribes pour décoller (en 40.000 signes),' *Revue d'esthétique*, Vols. 3/4, (1978) pp.34-35.

of reflection, collage, and transparency.'[13] Similarly, for John Stezaker, 'collage offers a perspective on the essential condition of the image in our culture: the existence of an image perpetually in relationship to one another.'[14] The splices, cuts and jumps in Waldrop's writing are, by and large, undetectable. The join is not registered at the poem's surface. Kurt Schwitters is also an important example. As Keith Waldrop notes, Schwitters' collages 'do not fit their elements into a story or "picture."' Hence, 'the elements remain formally suspended, visually in place while in most other ways out of place.'[15] The trick of collage consists also of never entirely suppressing the alterity of these elements reunited in a temporary composition.[16]

Such thinking ties in neatly with Waldrop's notion of the 'empty middle' so crucial to her poetics: that liminal zone between here and there, absence and presence, a borderline, a crossing, a trough. Crucially, however, such thinking is also emblematic of the reason why collage occupies such a privileged place at the centre of Waldrop's poetic method. Collage, that is, is one of the privileged methods precisely because it both performs and allows contiguity. In her essay, 'Thinking of Follows,' Waldrop suggests that 'collage, like fragmentation, allows you to frustrate the expectation of continuity, of step-by-step linearity.'[17] As a collage work takes shape, much textual movement is towards an equivocation between building and tearing; collage is the form, perhaps more than any other, of the art of the between. In the words of the French poet and friend of Waldrop's, Emmanuel Hocquard, collage corresponds to a 'surfing on pre-existing writings, passing between, creating other movements and other meanings from pre-existing materials.'[18] Collage is a form of relation but it is one where, as Joan Retallack outlines in her interview with Waldrop, such relation

---

[13] John Cage, 'Nicholas Zurbrugg Interviews John Cage,' *Eyeline*, No. 1 (May, 1987) p.6.
[14] David Lillington, 'A Conversation with John Stezaker,' in *Collage: Assembling Contemporary Art*, ed. Blanche Craig (London: Black Dog Publishing, 2008) p.31.
[15] Cooperman, 'Between Tongues.'
[16] For more on this, see also, Marjorie Perloff, 'Collage and Poetry,' *Encyclopedia of Aesthetics*, ed. Michael Kelly (New York: Oxford University Press, 1998) Vol. 1, pp.384-7.
[17] Waldrop, 'Thinking of Follows,' p.211.
[18] Emmanuel Hocquard, *Dix Leçons de Grammaire: Notes Préparatoires Pour Le Cours de Langage et Ecriture en Troisieme Année: Novembre 2001 – Janvier 2002* (Bordeaux: Ecole des Beaux Arts, 2003) p.17.

is premised on and by an 'epistemology of incompleteness' and the 'limits of knowing.'[19]

Brian Reed:

> Poundian collage is akin to the newsprint that Picasso frequently pasted to his canvasses during Cubism's founding 'analytic' phase. Both Pound's and Picasso's incorporations of borrowed text purport to offer a direct, indexical relationship between the artwork and the social world from which these materials have been drawn. The finished poem partakes in the ephemeral and the social with un-literary bluntness. Any attempts to praise it as a hermetic or autonomous text founder on its unlovely incorporation of mundane, often journalistic writing. As Peter Bürger would put it, such collage furthers the avant-garde project of breaking down the baleful distinction between art and 'life praxis' that prevails in late capitalism.
>
> Waldrop's version of collage [...] also recalls Cubist collage, albeit in a very different manner. It aspires to emulate the whole of a Cubist painting. In the years 1912-13, Picasso typically included not only found materials (chair caning, wallpaper, etc.) but also painted patches, stencilled letters, trompe l'oeil wood grain, and other traces of the artist's hand. In works such as 'Violin et partition', 'Tete d'homme au chapeau', and 'Bouteille et verre sur un guéridon', Picasso seeks not simply to undermine aesthetic autonomy but to issue a radical challenge to a complacent viewer's presumptions about how painting signifies. He quite literally deconstructs his art, employing shading that does not indicate depth, lines that do not suggest edges, superimposition that does not convey protension, and so forth [...] Similarly, Waldrop suggests that her borrowings have nothing naïve about them. She promises to manipulate, violate, crosscut, and otherwise render their unspoken assumptions overt. Pound's collage is evidentiary. Waldrop's is forensic.[20]

Throughout each of these determinations of collage, there is an implicit sense that the aesthetic of collage corresponds to a conceptual and linguistic notion of difference that harbours both a radical and

---

[19] Retallack, 'A Conversation,' p.341.
[20] Brian Reed, '"Splice of Life": Rosmarie Waldrop Renews Collage,' *How2*, Vol. 1, No. 8 (Fall, 2002), http://www.asu.edu/pipercwcenter/how2journal/archive/online_archive/v1_8_2002/current/readings/reed.htm, accessed 8 August 2012.

an ethical dimension. In 'The Author as Producer' Walter Benjamin suggests that one of the writer's most important strategic tasks is not so much to fill literary works with radical content but rather to develop the revolutionary potential of the forms themselves.[21] Equally, in its concerns with errancy the practice of collage is said to be ethical because, as Tim Woods notes, it 'develops as a challenge to find a methodology that maintains a respect for the heteronomy of our response to the other, and this search, in turn, concedes the deferment of one's own significance in the face of this obligation to otherness.'[22] In another register, collage corresponds to the ethical urgency Waldrop finds everywhere in notions of open form, non-narrative, contiguity, juxtaposition, conversation, questioning, approximation, silence, the white page and the responsibility of letting speech not complete itself. In very large measure, Waldrop's signature is the mark and movement of this open-endedness, the way various texts come and go, repeat, recycle. Writing becomes a practice of arrangement; specifically, it becomes an arrangement for that which never quite takes complete shape, which is never quite finished and often truant, and which reflects, at all times, John Ashbery's sense that any poem might have been differently written, written otherwise. 'Whenever I read a sentence, including a line of my own poetry,' Ashbery comments, 'I am beset by the idea that it could have been written any other way.'[23] For Waldrop, this is 'precisely what makes [poetry] a medium for thought, what makes it able to adumbrate (if not capture) transcendence, even the empty transcendence of nothingness. Rather than cause for lament, these moments where the void invades and erodes the word are epiphanies (uncomfortable, it is true) of language, of its essential tie to death, annihilation, nothingness.'[24]

Waldrop's sense of poetry here echoes Blanchot's sense of literature outlined in his essay, 'Literature and the Right to Death,' particularly in terms of what he defines there as the two 'slopes' of literature.[25] On one

---

[21] Walter Benjamin, 'The Author as Producer,' *Selected Writings, 1931-1934*, ed. Michael William Jennings (Cambridge, MA: Harvard University Press, 2005) pp.768-782.
[22] Tim Woods, *The Poetics of the Limit: Ethics and Politics in Modern and Contemporary American Poetry* (Basingstoke: Palgrave, 2002) p.68
[23] John Ashbery, *A Conversation with Kenneth Koch* (New York: Interview Press, 1965) n.p.
[24] Waldrop, *Lavish Absence*, p.83.
[25] Maurice Blanchot, 'Literature and the Right to Death,' *The Work of Fire*, trans. Charlotte Mandell (Stanford, CA: Stanford University Press, 1995) pp.300-344.

slope, understanding arises through conceptualisation. The ordering of the things into concepts is, according to Blanchot, a means of 'killing' them. Things are closed off, boundaries drawn and definitions declared and cast. The other slope corresponds to a form of literature that essentially lets things alone, lets them be as they are, what Simon Critchley terms 'letting things thing.'[26] In many ways, this other slope is the condition of ordinary things, things as they are, often messy, incomplete, contradictory, ambiguous, made up of bits and pieces, particularities, salvaged or recycled, perhaps, but not appropriated; the lines of a life; the stuff of things; the way one text is written, always, on top of another. 'I am,' Waldrop writes, 'everything I have ever read or written or thought. Language has no limits.'[27]

In this, for Waldrop one of the most important functions of poetry, of writing generally, of thinking and of living, is to 'foreground this awareness of the palimpsest as a method, using, transforming, "translating" parts of other works.'[28] As Waldrop notes, 'language comes not only with an infinite potential for new combinations, but also with a long history contained in it.'[29] This is an idea that reaches to the centre of Waldrop's poetic practice, and it is one Waldrop has expressed most directly in interview with Joan Retallack:

> We don't ever, quite, invent a wholly new world. Language exists already and potentially contains all that can be said in it. I think [Valéry's] 'the forest of language' is a very good metaphor. It's something we can move around in, there is so much of it. We never completely explore, let alone master. But we can discover things, make new connections et cetera. But we don't invent anything ex nihilo.[30]

Waldrop's method of collage—or what Marjorie Perloff has referred to as 'palimptextual' writing, whereby 'the palimtext retains vestiges of

---

[26] Simon Critchley, 'Tom McCarthy and Simon Critchley in conversation: Beckett, Adorno, Blanchot, Comedy, Death, and so on....,' Office of Anti-Matter, Austrian Cultural Institute, London (29 March 2001), http://voidmanufacturing.wordpress.com/2008/12/09/tom-mccarthy-and-simon-critchley-in-conversation-beckett-adorno-blanchot-comedy-death-and-so-on/, accessed 15 July 2012.
[27] Waldrop, 'The Ground is the Only Figure,' p.250.
[28] Waldrop, 'Form and Discontent,' p.204.
[29] Waldrop, 'Thinking of Follows,' p.207.
[30] Retallack, 'A Conversation,' p.366.

prior writings out of which it emerges. Or more accurately, it is the still-visible record of its responses to those earlier writings' – puts Gertrude Stein's sense of 'composition as explanation' into literal practice.[31] As Stein wrote, 'everything is the same except composition and as the composition is different and always going to be different everything is not the same.'[32] Hence, for Waldrop, there are 'always new forms, new structures, new perspectives, new ways of thinking, new ways of putting things together.'[33] It is, Waldrop argues, a primary task of poetic practice to attend these differences, to let them alone and 'let things thing'.

---

[31] Marjorie Perloff (ed.), *Postmodern Genres* (Norman and London: University of Oaklahoma Press, 1988) p.78.
[32] Gertrude Stein, 'Composition as Explanation,' *A Stein Reader*, ed. Ulla E. Dydo (Evanston, IL: Northwestern University Press, 1993) p.500.
[33] Retallack, *op. cit.*, p.367.

Between, Always

'If "about" anything, Waldrop's poetry is about how communication happens—how, through language, relationships—between people, between pronouns, between bodies and their shadows, between history and etymology—form temporary arrangements that dissolve and later reform in unfamiliar arrangements.'[1] For Waldrop poetry takes place in the spaces between words, in the interplay of these spaces. 'I am extremely interested in failure,' the speaker of the (prose-)poem 'Enigma Box' comments, '[t]he beginning of art lies next to the body, transitive fissure [...] what deviance from curved diameter and straightest line.'[2] For Waldrop, in other words, poetry is always disappearing elsewhere, moving off at a tangent, deviating in a direction difficult to follow and still harder to grasp. As a result, one of the central aspects around which Waldrop's poetry turns is the sense that language can be experienced only as fissure, gap, aperture, an 'empty middle' into which the possibility of meaning simultaneously both enters and escapes. Words double back, retrace their steps, and start over again, as if for the first time.

Much of Waldrop's sense of poetics here stems from her reading of the German-language avant-garde. As Waldrop puts it:

> When I started to write in English, in the mid-60s, my affinities were to the Black Mountain School, esp. Creeley, and some of the New York School (Barbara Guest and Ashbery). But I was also avidly reading the German-language avant-garde (the Vienna Group, esp. Ernst Jandl & Friederike Mayröcker, and the poets like Helmut Heissenbüttel, Franz Mon, and later Oskar Pastior).

Equally, Waldrop adds how:

> the most crucial encounter with writers my own age came with Claude Royet-Journoud and Anne-Marie Albiach in 1971 (and, somewhat later, Jacques Roubaud and Emmanuel Hocquard). The conversations with them clarified much of what I had been groping toward. I had begun avoiding metaphors in my poems or, rather, had begun pushing them out of the texture into the structure.[3]

---

[1] Emily Carr, 'Happily, Revision,' para. 8.
[2] Rosmarie Waldrop, *Blindsight* (New York: New Directions, 2003) p. 99.
[3] Email to author, 27 August, 2006.

In conversation, Waldrop has elaborated on this range of influences, commenting how her sense of not having a particular voice but trying to have many which blend, clash and form something of their own, a mesh as reverb, static, 'comes from farther back, from Keats' 'chameleon poet,' Musil's *Mann ohne Eigenschaften*, also Benn's 'Orangenstil,'—all segments around an empty center.'[4] In a letter to Richard Woodhouse, dated 27 October 1818, Keats refers to the 'chameleon poet' as a 'poetical character' which 'is not itself, it has no self. It is everything and nothing. It has no character. It enjoys light and shade.'[5] The chameleon poet, in other words, is an attempt to forge an identity out of 'uncertainties, Mysteries, doubts,' out of disinterestedness which is also an openness, what Grant F. Scott calls 'really a kind of celebration of the question of the world.'[6] Waldrop puts the point directly when she comments how, in a manner loosely similar to Blanchot's sense of the second slope of literature, Keats' notion of the chameleon poet is 'a challenge to closed systems.'[7] Equally, Gottfried Benn's sense of 'orangenstil' equates to a centripetal schema of writing where sentences do not follow any established, prescribed, or programmatic logic.

In various senses, Waldrop's books are not so much collections as multiple glimpses of the same thought, the same blind-spots. Just as one fragment cannot be taken in isolation from the sequence to which it belongs, so one work cannot be divorced from its relation to all the others. 'I can't imagine working without some counterpoint. And it usually comes from other writing.'[8]

'All words are ajar,' Waldrop writes in the tellingly titled and important essay 'Between, Always.'[9] Far from being closed units, words open onto a curvature of space that keeps them in relation, constantly sliding elsewhere in the instant of expression. Similarly, Waldrop's poetry taken as a whole is intersectional; each work operates in relation to the space left open by the previous one. Waldrop calls it 'an art of separation and fusion, of displacement and connection. For without our connecting them into a picture,' Waldrop continues, 'the dots are not even visible.' It is, Waldrop comments, 'an art of betweens.'[10]

[4] Email to author, 6 September 2006.
[5] John Keats, *Selected Letters of John Keats*, ed. Grant F. Scott (Cambridge, MA: Harvard University Press, 2005) pp.194-195.
[6] Grant F. Scott (ed.), *Selected Letters of John Keats*, p.xxxii.
[7] Waldrop, *Lavish Absence*, p.125.
[8] Hulme, 'Interview with Rosmarie Waldrop,' p.259.
[9] Waldrop, 'Between, Always,' p.272.
[10] ibid, p. 273.

'All words are ajar;' all writing opens onto the space of something other than itself. Waldrop comments, 'My sense of between is a sense of relation.'[11] 'I found it very exciting', she goes on to say, 'to discover how ubiquitous the image of the electromagnetic field is in the twentieth century. In the field, everything happens between; relation is everything.'[12] Waldrop's central frame of reference here is the work of the physicist, Alfred North Whitehead, particularly his proposition that the actual world, the world of experience, is composite, built up of 'occasions' rather than 'things'. The 'present experience is what I now am,' Whitehead writes. 'The soul is nothing else than the succession of my occasions of experience, extending from birth to the present moment. Now at this instant, I am the complete person embodying all these occasions. They are mine. On the other hand it is equally true that my immediate occasion of experience, at the present moment, is only one among the stream of occasions which constitutes my soul.'[13] Such occasions are what Whitehead refers to as the 'thread of life,' both personal and composite.[14]

Whitehead's theories have had a significant impact on Waldrop's poetic practice, but more for its general sense than its specific detail. Thus, while Waldrop has stressed on several occasions the importance of Whitehead, she also cites a range of other philosophical, scientific, and literary references and examples equally important to understanding the development of her sense of the between:

> Kurt Lewin describes mental states as balances of forces and vectors. Fenollosa examined the sentence and concluded: 'A true noun, an isolated thing, does not exist in nature. Things are only the terminal points, or rather the meeting points, of actions, cross-sections cut through actions, snapshots. Neither can a pure verb, an abstract motion, be possible in nature… Thing and action cannot be separated.' W.C. Williams says, 'the poem is a field of action.' Pound writes, 'the thing that matters in art is a sort of energy, a force transfusing, welding and unifying.' And of course Olson: 'At root (or stump) what is, is no longer THINGS but what happens BETWEEN things, these are the terms of the reality contemporary to us—and the

---

[11] Hulme, 'Interview with Rosmarie Waldrop,' p.77.
[12] ibid, p.77.
[13] Alfred North Whitehead, *Modes of Thought* (New York: Macmillan, 1938) p.163.
[14] ibid, p.161.

terms of what we are.'[15]

As Waldrop reminds readers in the essay 'Between, Always,' the title of one of her earliest poems written in the English language, collected in *The Aggressive Ways of the Casual Stranger*, was 'Between.'[16] On the face of it, the immediate context for that poem is Waldrop's sense of personal displacement following her move from Germany to America. As the speaker of the poem puts it, 'I'm not quite at home / on either side of the Atlantic.'[17] Yet what is actually most striking about the poem is less its biographical revelation as the way it suggests an aesthetic project tracing itself across the entirety of Waldrop's practice.

'[A]ware / I'm nowhere,' Waldrop goes on to write in that poem, 'I stand securely in a liquid plane / touched on all sides,' composite, occasioned, melded. Here, the 'occasion' corresponds to the 'fissure' into which the body, both of language and of the individual subject, diversifies and disperses. Indeed, in a poem which is concerned with issues of disarticulation and displacement, and which consists of 36 lines, the line at the poem's centre reads 'doesn't make you.' Far from being made by the poem, the speaking subject is actually undone by it, even as it is only on condition of this undoing that the subject appears in the poem at all. Much turns on this paradox, first expressed here and developed over the course of a life and a career. In order to be, speak, see, it is necessary that the sovereignty of the 'I', self-possession, be transgressed, opened, traced on other pages and in other words, that it be humble enough to home itself in the space of a question.

Another early poem, dedicated to Edmond Jabès and entitled 'Dark Octave,' develops this notion of constitutive negation. Beginning with the seemingly logical assertion that in order '[t]o see darkness / the eye withdraws from the light,' the poem proceeds to open this logic to its own internal suspension and, in so doing, spirals toward an implosion of the very act of seeing.[18] As light conditions seeing so the eye's withdrawal from light is also the eye's withdrawal from the economy of seeing; as the poem puts it, 'the eye / away from light / is eyeless.' Yet, instead of negating both the eye's function and the eye itself, it is precisely this condition of 'eyelessness' that, in the poem,

---

[15] Hulme, *op. cit.*, p.78.
[16] Waldrop, 'Between, Always,' p.265.
[17] Rosmarie Waldrop, 'Between,' *The Aggressive Ways of the Casual Stranger*, p.15.
[18] Waldrop, 'Dark Octave,' *The Aggressive Ways of the Casual Stranger*, p.34.

allows the eye to 'see' the invisible that is screened within the visible; not-seeing paradoxically manifests that which cannot be seen. Where the inability of the eye to detect darkness in light is classified in the poem as 'weakness,' the eye's turning away both from the light and from its own purposive meaning is figured as its 'power':

> its [the eyeless eye's] power is not-seeing
> and this not-seeing
> sees the night

Conceptualised in opposition to the more standard and culturally embedded notion of light being synonymous with knowledge, here the function of seeing is to proceed toward the perspective of non-perspective, things as they are; it is a way, of sorts, of 'letting the thing thing.' In the same way that in 'Between' the existence of the speaking subject was premised on its negative, in 'Dark Octave' darkness conditions both the presence of light and the possibility of seeing. As a result, in order to construct the lexicon of seeing Waldrop's poem tends toward the articulation of erasure. For instance, after an unambiguous warning not to dismiss darkness from the angle of vision ('do not dismiss your darkness / or you'll be left / with vision's / lesser angles,') 'Dark Octave' concludes with the lines:

> it
> occupies the eye entirely.

While everything that precedes this statement would seem to suggest that 'it' here relates to darkness, the anomalous isolation of 'it', together with its rhythmic interruption, complicates any such easy identification. Even if the 'it' is synonymous with darkness, the suggestion is that the impersonality of 'it' conditions the eye's angle of vision. Standing apart on the page from the rest of the poem the 'it' parallels the outlying shading to which it gives voice. In other words, where the depersonalised 'it' posits the 'unseeable' at the centre of seeing, its singular mark on the page at once both shadows and emphasises the blankness upon which it stands. In the same way that 'Between' placed the unmade at its literal centre, 'Dark Octave' is both focalised and made legible by the negative assertion—'is eyeless'—it inscribes at its centre. Common to both 'Between' and 'Dark Octave,' therefore, is the way each poem locates, at its respective centre, an empty middle. This is the shadow zone, the between point.

Stutter-Flow:
The Road Is Everywhere or Stop This Body

Published six years after *The Aggressive Ways of the Casual Stranger*, in her second full-length collection, *The Road is Everywhere or, Stop This Body*, Waldrop attempts to give voice to this empty middle by, as she puts it in her autobiography:

push[ing] at

THE BOUNDARIES OF THE SENTENCES,

sliding them together by letting the object of one sentence flip over into being the subject of the next.[1]

The Road Is Everywhere develops Waldrop's interest in prosody, particularly the sentence and the opening out of the line as a discrete unit into a rush of verse from one line to another, an experiment first begun proper in the long sequence which comprised the third and final part of *The Aggressive Ways of the Casual Stranger*, 'As If We Didn't Have to Talk.' Where in very early poems—such as 'Dark Octave'—lines tend to be end-stopped and complete syntactical units in themselves, in the poetry that followed Waldrop's research fellowship spent in Paris in 1970-1 and her meeting with Claude Royet-Journoud and Anne-Marie Albiach, lines begin to open out, double, tumble, one into the other, not always with clear connection or sequence. The dual rhythms of poetic form and life suddenly become more closely linked, more mutually reflective; the techniques, the form of living, and the living of form.

Although not published until 1978, the source material for *The Road Is Everywhere* stems from Waldrop's daily two hour commute from Providence to Wesleyan University between 1968 and 1970. As Steve Evans puts it, 'the seemingly endless hours spent in her Corvair gave Waldrop ample opportunity to study road signs (which are directly incorporated as textual elements in *The Road*) and to steep such abstract concepts as "circulation" and "traffic" (dictionary definitions of these words act as epigraphs for *The Road*) in concrete experience.'[2]

---

[1] Waldrop, *Ceci*, p. 83.
[2] Evans, 'Rosmarie Waldrop.'

Throughout the 80-part sequence that comprises *The Road is Everywhere* Waldrop is interested in exploring the tension between word, line, and silence by complicating the distinction between subject and object. As Waldrop puts it, 'I worked on making the object of one phrase flip over into being the subject of the next phrase without being repeated.'[3] Thus:

> weightless inside a density
> about to burn
> the air
> won't take the imprint we
> talk
> doubles the frequencies
> brought up short[4]

For Bruce Andrews, Waldrop's procedure here generates a series of displacements which chart 'a parallel between 2 senses of traffic: *the movement (of vehicles or pedestrians) through an area or along a route and the information or signals transmitted over a communication system: messages.*' And so, Andrews continues, 'we find content doubled, folded back into the constructed spaces of the page—first, revealing and articulating an experience of motion (and of mind/heart/memory/body/dream in motion through everyday traffic): second, doing the same for an experience of speech/words/meanings/writing as this second perspective actively unfolds from a transcription and embodiment of the first.'[5] Where traditional notions of verse (derived from the Latin *versus*, 'verse' denotes a line or a row, in particular a line of writing) figure the linear form as the turning of one line into the beginning of another, Waldrop's emphasis on both the doubling and the blurring of subject and object resituates this 'turning' from a 'turning toward' to a 'turning away.'[6]

---

[3] Waldrop, 'Thinking of Follows,' p.209.
[4] Waldrop, *The Road is Everywhere or, Stop This Body* (Columbia, MI: Open Places, 1978), p.13.
[5] Bruce Andrews, 'The Hum of Words,' in Bruce Andrews and Charles Bernstein (eds.), *The L=A=N=G=U=A=G=E Book* (Carbondale and Edwardsville: Southern Illinois University Press, 1984) p.277.
[6] The *Oxford English Dictionary* defines 'verse' as '[a] succession of words arranged according to natural or recognised rules of prosody and forming a complete metrical line; one of the lines of a poem or piece of versification.' *Oxford English Dictionary*, Vol. XII (London: Oxford University Press, 1970) p. 141.

Stutter-Flow

In her doctoral dissertation, Waldrop outlines the ways in which Helmut Heisenbüttel argues that overturning 'the subject-predicate formula of Western languages is one of the most important tasks of the poets.'[7] Heisenbüttel might not be that well known in the English-speaking world, but his poetics are hugely influential on Waldrop, particularly in terms of the formal and thematic importance she ascribes to innovations with syntax. As Waldrop quotes Heisenbüttel:

> The experience which is talked about is outside the unequivocal subject-object relation. Only the formulation that leaves one of the parts in the old basic model open can say something about it. Contexts are not formed by systematic logical-syntactical interweaving, but by secondary meanings, by ambiguities that result from the weather-beaten syntax.[8]

Throughout *The Road is Everywhere* the brevity of the verse line combined with spiralling sentences produces a syntax that is frequently at odds with itself. As the first sequence reads:

> exaggeration of a curve
> exchanges
> time and again
> beside you in the car
> pieces the road together
> with night moisture
> the force of would-be sleep
> beats through our bodies
> denied their liquid depth
> toward the always dangerous next
> dawn bleeds its sequence
> of ready signs[9]

On the one hand, in the absence of punctuation, the line breaks prevent the structural combination of language, so that the sequence's legibility is, to a greater or lesser extent, always already fractured. Each line can be read neither as a complete unit in itself nor as a clearly defined constitutive part of a whole. Rather the constant turning from

---

[7] Waldrop, *Against Language?*, p.50.
[8] Helmut Heisenbüttel, *Über Literatur* (Olten: Walter, 1966), p.223; quoted in Waldrop, *Against Language?*, p.50.
[9] Waldrop, *The Road is Everywhere*, p.1.

and displacement of subject and object inscribes, at the level of both individual line and the sequence as a whole, a constant interruption into the text. The curve with which the sequence begins is simply an arc of exchangeability that shifts without obvious explanation into an unnamed presence within a car, a road, night moisture, an abstract energy resembling sleep and so on. At the same time, however, the opposite is also the case. Structure is cast also from extreme feverishness. The ability of Waldrop's sequence to maintain two contradictory impulses at the same time is one of its most significant achievements. It manages to maintain this simultaneity largely because while the absence of punctuation combined with the uncertainty of the syntactical relation interrupts narrativity, it also at the same time propels one line into the next. In this sense, each phrase streams into the next to the extent that it is far from clear where one phrase ends and another begins. As Waldrop comments of the sequence in interview:

> [t]he object of one sentence is always also the subject of the next, so that there is no complete sentence, but each poem as a whole becomes one continuous, strangely shifting, ungrammatical sentence.[10]

On one level, in the passage above it would appear that the curve (object of the first line) becomes the unspoken subject of the entire rest of the sequence. Yet, on another level, the curve may actually turn into the car of the fourth line, so that the car is effectively the thing that pieces the road together with night moisture while that night moisture is actually the force of would-be sleep and would-be sleep is what beats through the bodies. Both readings are possible just as the sequence is, at one and the same time, both fragmented and flowing.

For Waldrop, though, the point of this interplay and doubling has less to do with trying to reconstruct a specific and/or credible textual reading than it does with finding a method of writing that multiplies possible readings such that what comes into focus is both a formal and semantic ambiguity. If everything unravels into everything, then, at the same time, everything also unravels into nothing and nothing into everything; in Waldrop's terms: 'if everything is possible, nothing is,' and vice versa.[11] The sequence resituates the empty middle from the

---

[10] Joan Retallack, 'A Conversation with Rosmarie Waldrop,' p. 339.
[11] ibid, p. 365.

centre of the text to the margins, into the beginning and end of lines, that constantly sliding gap between subject and object. The poem's first word, 'exaggeration,' is particularly resonant in this regard. The structural and thematic curve exceeds the bounds of signification even as it gives voice to this excess in the way each line runs over into the next in a manner far more complicated than examples of enjambment. Throughout the sequence language, perception, and experience are sensed only as interchange and variation.

This variation only multiplies throughout the course of the sequence. As each of the poem's lines and syntactical units require a double reading—or perhaps better, a reading that doubles itself, that shifts backwards, away from the end of each line—so sequential development, narrativity, is turned on its head. The poem, in other words, repeatedly exceeds its own frame of reference. '[P]resence every / day shifts unceasingly' in the same way that all sequences and perspectives, by their very nature, shift. In its turning inside out, then:

>   what you took for granted
>   rises from the wrong end
>
>   of a sentence and from then on
>   it's   DETOUR
>
>
>   after
>   DETOUR [12]

Nothing comes, nothing moves, and yet, at the same time, everything does. Words and phrases leak into 'ready signs' although they do not form them. When the distinction between subject and object is no longer distinct, ambiguities of meaning are amplified and signs lack clear markers. In this way, the word 'exaggeration' serves the semantic function of establishing an irreducible excess at the very outset of the poem that is mimed throughout by the poem's spiralling syntax. In its movement back and forth, the poem is sent simultaneously back into and outside itself. What is exaggerated, which is to say, what the poem fails to arrest, to stabilise into either distinct image or discrete

---
[12] Waldrop, *The Road is Everywhere*, p.5.

poetic unit, is precisely this constant 'traffic', 'the effect of hurtling down main-clause highway at breakneck speed.'[13] Thus for Bruce Andrews the poem 'frame[s] and reframe[s] the flows around us, and the explosions which fracture the present. Body becomes its own flow; the person is a matrix of those flows & exchanges & messages. Person is a communicative system, a traffic.'[14] While the poem is constantly rushing toward 'the shock of the "outside"' the poem constantly runs into the difficulty of stopping, standing still, getting bearings.[15] '[S]kin / flaunts its refusal / to harden into / durability' just as the poem's final sequence concludes with 'eyes open on / the constant disappearing / translating / one measurement / into another.'[16] There are no exits, just a constant going, and the rush of frameworks constitutes its acuteness.

---

[13] Waldrop, 'Thinking of Follows,' p.209.
[14] Andrews, 'The Hum of Words,' p.277.
[15] Waldrop, *The Road is Everywhere*, p.79.
[16] ibid, p.80.

Linearity in Pieces: *Nothing Has Changed*

Composed of thirty-five sections, ranging from three to ten lines in length, Waldrop's 1975 sequence *Nothing Has Changed* repeatedly exemplifies this disruption at each of the units of line, phrase, fragment and whole. Ostensibly a speculative sequence exploring proximity and distance, presence and absence, attraction and separation, speech and silence, *Nothing Has Changed* ultimately settles into the non-space of an interval that, from the very outset, is figured as '[a] sort of empty number / [...] / never more present' yet 'all you / around you.'[1] Throughout the sequence the poem's empty number is that which is, at the same time, both excessively present and radically non-present. On the one hand, if the empty number is 'all you' then this non-specifiable blankness is not only what the 'you' contains but also what names it. On the other hand, if it is also that which is 'around you' then it is that which lies beyond the 'you.' As a result, the 'empty number' both codifies the 'you' (the song) and opens up a conceptual space into which it (the you, the song) disappears. The poem, in other words, is formed by emptying; the substance of the poem becomes the manner in which substance flows out.

This paradoxical movement around which *Nothing Has Changed* repeatedly moves is perhaps most clearly illustrated by the poem's fourteenth section:

> I can't stand with
> waiting to be present
> not only as it would have been
> decision out of reach
> and because I openly
> you too lost
> in waiting[2]

Here waiting both defers and deforms any clear identity of 'I' and 'you.' Throughout *Nothing Has Changed* pronouns merge into other pronouns to such an extent that it is impossible to identify a specific voice or subject behind the poem. In certain respects, the poem's

---

[1] Rosmarie Waldrop, 'Nothing Has Changed,' *Living Hand* 4 (Winter 1975), p.81 [pp.74-94]; later published as *Nothing Has Changed* (Windsor, VT: Awede Press, 1981).
[2] ibid, p.81.

composite structure complicates, no doubt deliberately, the possibility of identifying the voice of one section with that of another. In other respects, though, the constant slippages of register between I, you, he, she, and we, sometimes within the space of a single fragment, complicate any clear sense of each as a discrete subject by diffusing them across an impersonal lexicon of merging and perpetual non-coincidence. For instance, as section four reads:

> parallel open so we could
> against one another
> turn
> you know there is
> between attention
> a place never direct
> nor an object to stay near
> impersonal attention you don't with
> extreme[3]

and section twenty-four:

> you can't make this distinction
> it's very strong and nothing hinders
> because your presence in its
> always I mean
> dispersing always
> and separating[4]

Taken together, these fragments point toward the constant shifting of pronouns. In section four, the exposure of 'I' to 'you' and vice versa does not so much result in any kind of convergence into a 'we' as it does a kind of impersonal separation; between 'you' and 'I' 'a place never direct / nor an object to stay near;' between 'you' and 'I' there is neither subject nor object. Rather, there is only an ambiguous attention spilling into an 'extreme' elsewhere, fragmenting and shifting. Such a conceptual reading is paralleled by the fragment's formal structure of syntactical subversion and discontinuity. Where the open equivalence between 'you' and 'I' renders any 'we' anonymous, the complication of syntax results in an increasingly 'extreme' refusal of both semantic continuity and correspondence.

---

[3] ibid, p.76.
[4] ibid, p.86.

At the 'extreme' point disconnection occurs. The 'extreme' toward which the fragment points and ultimately ends becomes the very essence of the fragment, the point around which the entire sequence is gathered. As the final two lines from the twenty-seventh fragment clarifies:

> when you're there it's not quite
> what you see once and for all[5]

Things can be named, neither with consistency nor with confidence. Rather:

> what makes you
> it's between us
> it's what[6]

As with much of the poem, it is not clear here whether 'what' functions as an interrogative, indefinite or relative pronoun. Is the first line to be read as a question (in the sense of, what makes you?) or a statement (that which makes you)? Is the second line a continuation of the first (that which makes you is that which is between us) or does it respond by suggesting what is 'between us' is what 'makes you'? Nor is it clear whether the third line asks what it is that is 'between us' that 'makes you,' or whether it proposes that what is 'between us' is simply that, the indirect and largely non-specifiable space of 'what'. Equally, it may be, simply, a condensed repetition of the first two lines, in the sense that it repeats the notion that 'you' is constructed by that which exists in between 'you' and 'I' ('us').

All this said, however, it might well be that to distinguish between such readings is perhaps to miss the point of the poem. What matters is not trying to pin the poem down but paying attention to the various ways in which the poem complicates the practice of reading. 'Give back what disappears,' Waldrop writes in the sixth fragment, 'as if a detour in forgetting / could.'[7] Compacted, circuitous, and complicated, both this fragment and the poem as a whole mime the dispossession implied by the opening demand to 'give back' (after all, there is no need to demand what one already has). At the same time, however,

---
[5] ibid, p.87.
[6] ibid, p.79.
[7] ibid, p.77.

the shifting abbreviation that characterises *Nothing Has Changed* gives back precisely 'what' it demands, namely a sense that something here is disappearing, not quite said, not quite formed.

Prose Poems

Where Waldrop's initial publications 'propose a grammar in which subject and object function are not fixed [...], where there is no hierarchy of main and subordinate clauses, but a fluid and constant alteration' in order to give early voice to the excluded middle, in subsequent collections Waldrop's primary staging ground for her formal and conceptual interests has been prose. In particular, Waldrop's central preoccupation has been with experimenting with ways in which to open out the closed unit of the propositional sentence.

In the elliptical essay, 'Why Do I Write Prose Poems', Waldrop outlines how her movement away from the fractured line of verse towards a more expansive prose poetry corresponded with a desire for 'complex sentences, for the possibility of digression, for space,' which Waldrop goes on to call the 'space of a different, less linear movement.'[1]

> I gave up stress for distress [...] the distress of lacking coordinates, of the unstructured space of prose, the unchartered territory of the page. The excitement and terror of the open. Versus the challenge of closure: in the complete sentence and, extreme, in the proposition.[2]

'Verse,' Waldrop writes, 'refuses to fill up all of the available space of the page. Even if the words celebrate what is (which mine usually don't), each line acknowledges what is not. It makes manifest that "to create is to make a pact with nothingness" (Clark Coolidge). Or, as Heather McHugh put it, "[poetry] is the very art of turnings, toward the white frame of the page, toward the unsung, toward the vacancy made visible, that worldlessness in which our words are couched."'[3]

Prose, on the other hand, shifts the discontinuities, sites of reference and fissures, around which Waldrop's writing revolves from the outside to the inside, away from the highly visible jagged edges of verse to the site of the sentence. It was a shift that began to govern Waldrop's poetics more and more after her experiments with subject-object clauses in her early collections. As Waldrop comments, after *The Road is Everywhere*:

---

[1] Waldrop, 'Why Do I Write Prose Poems,' *Dissonance*, p.261.
[2] ibid, p.262.
[3] Rosmarie Waldrop, 'Response,' *Double Room: A Journal of Prose Poetry and Flash Fiction*, Issue 1 (Fall 2002/Winter 2003), http://doubleroomjournal.com/issue_one/RW_ResBio.html, accessed 21 April 2010.

> I began to long for subordinate clauses, complex sentences. So I turned to writing prose poems. I became fascinated by Wittgenstein and by the form of the proposition because of its extreme closure. This was a challenge after working toward opening the boundaries of the sentence by sliding sentences together or by fragmentation. I accepted the complete sentence (most of the time) and tried to subvert its closure and logic from the inside, by constantly sliding between frames of reference.[4]

In his 1977 essay, 'The New Sentence,' Ron Silliman describes the sentence, simply, as 'a unit of measure'. Sentence structure, Silliman adds, 'is altered for torque, or increased polysemy/ambiguity' and by way of which syllogistic movement is restricted. 'The limiting of syllogistic movement,' Silliman suggests, 'keeps the reader's attention at or very close to the level of language, that is, most often at the sentence level or below.'[5] And as Silliman goes on to summarise, 'the new sentence is a decidedly contextual object. Its effects occur as much between, as within, sentences. Thus it reveals that the blank space, between words or sentences, is much more than the 27th letter of the alphabet. It is beginning to explore and articulate just what those hidden capacities might be.'[6]

Through such exploration, what particularly interests Waldrop is the bluff where prose and poetry meet, or, more properly, where the one falls into the other, prose into poetry and poetry into prose. It is what Waldrop refers to as the 'between-genre,' such that 'the prose paragraph has a spaciousness where form can prove "a center around which, not a box within which."'[7] As Silliman puts it, 'the paragraph is a unit of quantity, not logic or argument.'[8]

Here syntax becomes structure and form, a line of transition, both propinquity and shift, the way one word slides into another, the way a sentence emerges and spaces itself; intervals, regular or otherwise. In other words, grammatical structure becomes syntactic, it becomes

---

[4] Waldrop, 'Thinking of Follows,' p.210.
[5] Ron Silliman, *The New Sentence* (New York: Roof Books, 1989) p.91.
[6] ibid, p.92.
[7] Rob Mclennan, '12 or 20 Questions with Rosmarie Waldrop,' *Rob Mclennan's Blog*, 11 January 2008, http://robmclennan.blogspot.co.uk/2008/01/rosmarie-waldrop-was-born-in-kitzingen.html, accessed 4 June 2012.
[8] Silliman, *op. cit.*, p.91.

what Marjorie Perloff refers to as 'structures of subordination rather than coordination.'[9] Even as phrases combine and pile, such discursive development is non-narrative. It does not so much build by degrees as by shards, discrete, discreet. Grammar becomes the space and site of contiguity, a configuration. Not so much a yoking as sightlines of crossing. 'Walking the space of a line,' Waldrop calls it, 'a phrase. As if finding it. As grammar of motion.'[10]

Such movement or crossing also functions to realise Waldrop's attempt to sidestep causality, rationality, and to construct instead a grammar and a language which is, first and foremost, contiguous rather than relational. 'My sequences,' Waldrop comments, 'make a tease of narrative. They have a narrative structure, but I don't really wrap anything up.'[11]

The sequence, 'Hölderlin Hybrids', from *Blindsight*, is a case in point:

> Here I work toward. A kind of elegy. Here a strange ceiling. "Earth fills his mouth." I would look at you. And write you. A spell but slack at the edge. And in the door where I stand your voice goes. Hollow.[12]

The full-stop becomes a rhythmic device. Connections and continuities, sometimes strange, sometimes less so, suggest themselves, but they do so only at the elision of syntax and punctuation. Full-stops act as a caesura, 'another empty center' and disjoint as much as they structure and build by degrees.[13] There is, for example, no necessary, or necessarily clear, connection between 'Here I work toward' and 'A kind of elegy', although there may be, and perhaps is, but the connection is divided and this full-stop is the fault line, the 'strange ceiling,' *by way of which* the poem is, first and foremost, experienced. As the quotation marks in the above passage make explicit, more than one text is at stake here, and thus more than one reading; all 'slack at the edge' just as all folds are numerous, both threshold and hollow. 'Tension,' Waldrop writes,

---

[9] Marjorie Perloff, 'Towards a Wittgensteinian Poetics,' *Contemporary Literature*, Vol. 33, No. 2, Special Issue: American Poetry of the 1980s (Summer 1992) p.206 [pp.191-213].
[10] Waldrop, 'The Ground is the Only Figure,' p.245.
[11] Demick, 'An Interview with Keith and Rosmarie Waldrop.'
[12] Waldrop, *Blindsight*, p.3.
[13] Waldrop, 'The Ground is the Only Figure,' p.250.

'is also one of the ways we can talk about rhythm. As long as you write in a regular meter you can talk about rhythm in terms of the tension between the meter and "normal" speech. In free verse, in terms of the tension between line and sentence. But in prose poems? I've recently used periods as rhythmic markers rather than, or in addition to, using them as grammatical markers: "How the words are. Suspended around you."'[14]

In this sense, Waldrop's use of punctuation in her prose sequences also functions to realise her attempt to sidestep causality, rationality, and to construct instead a grammar and a language which is, first and foremost, contiguous rather than relational. 'My sequences,' Waldrop comments, 'make a tease of narrative. They have a narrative structure, but I don't really wrap anything up.'[15] Elsewhere Waldrop notes how 'perhaps the greatest challenge of the prose poem [...] is to compensate for the absence of the margin. I try to place the margin, the emptiness inside the text. I cultivate cuts, discontinuity, leaps, shifts of reference etc. "Gap gardening," I have called it, and my main tool for it is collage,'[16] 'the unbedding of the always.'[17]

Waldrop's 1993 work, *Lawn of Excluded Middle* is exemplary in this regard.

---

[14] Hulme, 'Interview with Rosmarie Waldrop,' p.79.
[15] Demick, 'An Interview with Keith and Rosmarie Waldrop.'
[16] Rosmarie Waldrop, 'Response,' *Double Room: A Journal of Prose Poetry and Flash Fiction*, http://doubleroomjournal.com/issue_one/RW_ResBio.html, accessed 8 August 2012.
[17] Pam Rehm, quoted by Waldrop in 'The Ground is the Only Figure,' p.242.

Short Circuits

In the deliberately fragmentary essay 'Alarms and Excursions'—which loosely uses the structure of the Elizabethan stage term, 'alarums and excursions', denoting off-stage noise and commotion that interrupts the main action, excursion here denoting 'aside' in the sense of 'sally, sortie, raid'—Waldrop argues that 'it is one of the important tasks of poems to short-circuit the transparency that words have for the signified and which is usually considered their advantage for practical uses.'[1] For Waldrop, poetry is not so much directed by the pursuit of individual or common meaning as by the impractical, which is to say, the aporia of practice. Waldrop's poetry aims for what might be termed a laying bare of language, a language which precedes social communication and which, in a phrase that has circulated throughout Waldrop's various writings, constitutes 'another language', that most simple of languages that remains when notions of meaning or intention—transfer, transmission—are no longer a primary concern.

The gap between theory and practice, however, is often larger than footfall and, as Waldrop puts it in the published version of her doctoral thesis, *Against Language*, 'our idea of what is simple [...] is still the beginning of the inexpressible.'[2] This contradiction between expression and inexpression, between trying to show the inexpressible as inexpressible, in words, has a long literary and philosophical history, and it is a question which holds a pivotal role at the centre of Waldrop's poetics. In *Immemorial Silence* Karmen MacKendrick notes how 'the concern with the limits of language is a tradition with multiple roots: we find it in ancient mysticism as the "ineffable," in negative theology as the unnamable, in the Nietzschean warning that grammar seduces us into a belief in metaphysics, even in the Wittgensteinian warning that philosophy, being all language games, must not infrequently remain silent.'[3] Indeed, as Ludwig Wittgenstein famously cautioned in the seventh section of the *Tractatus*, 'whereof one cannot speak, thereof one must be silent.'[4] Yet, in the context of Waldrop's response to these

---

[1] Waldrop, 'Alarms and Excursions,' p.179.
[2] Rosmarie Waldrop, *Against Language?*, p.16.
[3] Karmen MacKendrick, *Immemorial Silence* (Albany, NY: State University of New York Press, 2001) p.3.
[4] Ludwig Wittgenstein, *Tractatus Logico-Philosophicus*, trans. D.F. Pears and B.F. McGuinness (London: Routledge, 1961), p.151.

questions, it might be just as well to remember Maurice Blanchot's rejoinder that 'to be silent is still to speak. Silence is impossible.'[5]

At issue here is a methodological problem. How, for instance, is 'simple' language to be expressed *as such*? And more than that, given the difficult or non-standard form such a language will take necessarily, how might such a simple language relate to wider social or public experience? How, in other words, might such a poetic be read?

The earliest response Waldrop gives to this methodological problem is to suggest that 'the way to the ineffable does not [...] go via the infinite and supremely meaningful but via the infinitesimal where all meaning ceases.'[6] In order to express the inexpressible, Waldrop suggests, it is necessary for form and content, including the standard critical distinction between the two, to be undone. For Waldrop, such an unravelling primarily directs language not so much from the point of view of meaning but from delirium. As Waldrop points out, delirium signifies 'a wandering from the *lira*, from the rut,' which is to say, it suggests a diversion from rules, regulations, systems and laws, those lines and lessons which fabricate life, which cover its insufficiency, its lack.[7] And, in various senses, Waldrop's poetry is delirious; it makes of this wandering its groundless matter.

In another register, such a poetics might be understood as a poetics of the 'neuter', in the particular sense given to that word by Maurice Blanchot. 'The neuter,' Blanchot writes, 'supposes a relation depending neither on objective conditions nor on subjective dispositions.'[8] It is, rather, the *between point* of view, that fault line upon which Waldrop's sense of poetics both rests and makes itself.

On this analogy, the task of poetry is to make of gaps both its form and function; in the space of the unspoken, Waldrop maintains, lies the motivation for thought: 'in the gaps we might get hints of much that has to be left unsaid—but should be thought about.'[9] In her early work, Waldrop predominantly attempts this task by way of a fractural disturbance of the poetic line: pared down words hang suspended across the grain of a page that quietly threatens to submerge them, while the

---

[5] Maurice Blanchot, *The Writing of the Disaster*, trans. Ann Smock (Lincoln and London: University of Nebsraska Press, 1995), p.10.
[6] Waldrop, *Against Language?*, p.17.
[7] ibid, p.30.
[8] Blanchot, *The Infinite Conversation*, p. 299.
[9] Retallack, 'A Conversation with Rosmarie Waldrop,' p.341.

mutation of object into subject has the (delirious) effect of abandoning the text to the possibility of multiple readings. In this regard Waldrop's turn to the prose fragment would appear to mark something of a formal and thematic departure. At the very least, it could be argued that the visual block-form of a prose fragment effectively disguises the space of disappearance her early work was so intent on visually displaying. Yet just as the expression of the inexpressible inevitably turns around what has not been said, so it is precisely by way of non-appearance that, across the prose fragments, disappearance actually comes into view. Where the line-break places the edge of the text in a legible physical contact with the white space that surrounds it, the prose fragment reveals emptiness as that of which it constantly loses sight. Emptiness, in other words, appears as plenitude, within the linguistic mark that contradicts it. Thus, while Waldrop's direct assertion in the first fragment of *Lawn of Excluded Middle* that she places an 'empty space [...] at the centre of each poem'[10] would appear to contradict that emptiness by substantiating it in the form of an unequivocal statement, it is in fact only on condition of this literal contradiction that emptiness enters the poem at all.

Essentially placeless, emptiness is not of the order of that which can be placed either here or there. Like Blanchot's neuter, it is the between point. As a result, then, to assert that one places an empty space is actually to assert very little. Once emptiness becomes sited it is no longer emptiness; once it is no longer emptiness, the statement that asserts it places emptiness at its centre becomes little more than a contradiction in terms.

In this sense, it is precisely the incongruity of the poem's form to its function, the fact that it strikes a discordant note, that marks out the prose form as the exemplary staging ground of the empty centre. The contradiction between the sequential referentiality of prose and the poem's subject matter *pronounces* silence precisely because it effaces its articulation at every turn. By shifting silence from the margins of the text to its textual centre, the sentence becomes both ground and figure. Similarly, because of the compacted density of its textual presentation, the prose fragment always already mimes emptiness at its very surface. Ink stretches from justified margin to justified margin, covering the page only with a proliferation of graphical marks. Before structures of

---

[10] Waldrop, *Lawn of Excluded Middle*, p. 14.

signification reconnect these markings, in other words, each grapheme is simply a *pre-text* of variously patterned spots of ink. This is the first experience of the poem. Prior to reading, the encounter with the poem takes place first and foremost with its general appearance. What this suggests is that the initial condition of the poem is, in fact, non-semantic. It bears stressing that for Waldrop a poem is as much a physical entity as it is a linguistic unit, which is to say, for Waldrop, the physical image of the poem is as much a part of the poem as its text.

Waldrop's 1990 volume, *Peculiar Motions*, is a case in point. Composed of ten poems, the volume also includes four so-called 'S/kins' printed on vellum that intersect and intervene with the legibility of the book's text. Each vellum both closes off and opens onto the poem it interleaves; they disrupt the reading process even as they afford a glimpse of the text they veil. As the artist of the 'S/kins,' Jennifer Macdonald, comments:

> these images intersect the poetry by way of metaphor and movement [...] As a permeable membrane, the *S/kins* intervene as a moment of passage between pages, alternately veiling and revealing the language below.[11]

Here the inclusion of vellum both redoubles the surface image of the poem on the page, and makes of this redoubling a central part of the reading process. In order to read *Peculiar Motions*, therefore, in order to read its text, it is necessary to interact with its physical space as book, with the alternations of text and texture, presentation and effacement.

Similarly, and to draw the focus back toward *Lawn of Excluded Middle*, the typographical presentation of each prose fragment on a separate folio does not so much foreground the large blank space that surrounds the prose above and below as emphasise the clearly defined concentration of ink on the page. In other words, the surface image of ink is that which is immediately striking. At the same time, however, that surface image is also that which is immediately blinding. The reader first encounters the poem from a physical distance, in the turning of a page, with pinched hand and crease of spine, the texture of finger and folio, where the out of focus eye, detached from the definite, catches a glimpse only of the blurred generality of the poem's

---

[11] Jennifer Macdonald, 'S/kins,' in Rosmarie Waldrop, *Peculiar Motions* (Berkeley, CA: Kelsey St. Press, 1990) p.11.

overall shape. This image is the text's question, the one it both sounds and muddles at every turn. The eye is not so much directed to the particulars of linguistic units as it is to the space between words, the diversions of the text's internal blank spaces that set one graphic mark apart from another. In other words, the eye does not so much see the poem as it does its internal fissures. As a consequence, and even if the duration of this initial indirection of focus is minute to the extent of being largely unconscious, *in the first instance* the poem's text (its language) is transmitted simply as pre-text (image). As Waldrop put it in the early poem, 'Dark Octave,' the power of the eyeless eye lay precisely in its ability to 'not see', so each poem signifies by way of its pre-grammatological appearance.[12] This is particularly apposite of the prose poem in the sense that its dense block structure renders this pre-grammar 'shadow zone' acutely visible. As Waldrop writes, 'the eye is a camera, room for everything that is to enter, like the cylinder called the satisfaction of hollow space;' the image of the poem subsists as the hollow space into which, slipping, the eye spirals.[13]

None of this is intended to suggest that the semantic element of each prose poem is subordinate to the physical presentation of graphemes. The point, simply, is that, for Waldrop, 'reference is secondary' to the physical structure of the poem.[14] 'The poem,' she comments, 'works by indirection' and the surface is a pivotal aspect of reading this indirection.[15] Words are neither means of entry nor indicative markers of functional application. Rather, as the syntactically separated yet simultaneously juxtaposed 'life' and 'still' would appear to suggest in *Lawn of Excluded Middle*'s second section, units of language reveal only a still life *image*, life prior to perception, an eye dissociated from function. There is no getting at what, if anything, lies behind the word. And yet, at the same time, it is only on account of this obstinate illegibility that, paradoxically, 'the mind' perceives 'depth.'[16] The opacity of the surface is what renders the sheer extent of the surface 'translucent.'[17] Or again: because the surface is impenetrable, the surface extends in all directions. Surface is deep; it stretches all the way down

---

[12] Waldrop, 'Dark Octave,' p.34.
[13] Waldrop, *Lawn of Excluded Middle*, p.8.
[14] Waldrop, 'Alarms and Excursions,' p.54.
[15] ibid, p.54.
[16] Waldrop, *Lawn*, p.7.
[17] ibid, p.7.

to the bareness of bones, the disembodied cylinder struck through with a hollow space it can neither contain nor obtain. It disappears there, back into the plane of itself. As with Blanchot's notion of the neuter, the poem's impermeable surface is simply a dissipating 'phrase [...] without predicate.'[18] Language intends 'disappearance by approaching it,' by disappearing in the movement of approach.[19]

At each of the levels of pre-text (physical image) and text (syntactical image), then, *Lawn of Excluded Middle* at all times mimes the dissolution of both substance and subject. Neither here nor there, positive nor negative, the work of the poem takes place only in the non-space of elsewhere. In this sense, the taking place of the poem— its work—would be nothing other than the 'lawn of excluded middle' itself. Outside the 'venerable old law of logic' that pits truth against falsity, light against dark, male against female, which is to say, outside the oppositional structure of signification, the lawn of excluded middle is a point of crossing and doubling back, a muddle, a muddying.[20] To put it another way, the lawn of excluded middle exposes the notion of limit to the point at which signification blurs, appearing in and as that blurring, a double movement of taking place and suspending. As Deborah Meadows clarifies:

> at the syntax level, the sentence is an axiomatic structure that both: 1. annihilates what it uses as a vehicle of expression, of evidence; and 2. restores and preserves its vehicle as an inseparable structure of meaning, of evidence. Waldrop shows us the gap between language as a self-referential system and experience.[21]

Read in this way, the constantly redoubling movement of the sentence in *Lawn of Excluded Middle* mirrors the exigency of its physical form: both make of emptiness their paradoxical substance. As section twenty six reads:

---

[18] ibid, p.7.
[19] ibid, p.7.
[20] ibid, p.68.
[21] Deborah Meadows, 'Rosmarie Waldrop and the Poetics of Embodied Philosophy,' *How2*, Vol. 1, No. 8 (Fall, 2002), http://www.asu.edu/ pipercwcenter/how2journal/archive/online_archive/v1_8_2002/current/readings/ meadows.htm, 20 December 2010.

I wanted to settle down on a surface, a map perhaps, where my near-sightedness might help me see the facts. But grammar is deep. Even though it only describes, it submerges the mind in a maelstrom without discernible bottom, the dimensions of possibles swirling over the fixed edge of nothingness.[22]

Depth of surface is precisely that which prevents the mapping of limits, the related processes of legislation and legitimation. It disappears into its own far-flung submergence, its distance from presence, its immeasurable emptiness. The lawn of excluded middle is this immeasurability, a shadow zone, site of difference. As a result, the lawn of excluded middle simultaneously reflects and posits what is referred to as 'an alternate, less linear logic,' which is to say, a 'logic' that is 'logical' only insofar as it pertains to a governable law of self-cancellation.[23] The fracture of nothingness it opens is the interminable fissure into which it slips. 'The mistake,' Waldrop writes, 'is to look for explanations where we should just watch the slow fuse burning [...] What we let go we let go.'[24] Both indifferent and in-difference, the logic of the lawn of excluded middle here is simply the passivity of its letting go: of logic but also of its own self-identity as that which 'lets go'. 'The meaning of certainty is getting burned' whereby 'getting burned' should be understood also in the sense of 'put upon,' 'had,' 'tricked,' 'taken in,' 'deceived'.[25]

Always self-divided, in its constant redoubling, the alternate logic of the lawn of excluded middle functions in a manner similar to notions of irony and scepticism. As Paul de Man discusses in 'The Rhetoric of Temporality', irony is duplicitous and always different from itself. 'Curiously enough,' de Man writes, 'it seems to be only in describing a mode of language which does not mean what it says that one can actually say what one means.'[26] Ironic discourse is divided, always different-from-itself. 'If the "possibility" of writing is linked to the "possibility" of irony,' Blanchot suggests, 'then we understand why one and the other are always disappointing: it is impossible to lay claim to either; both exclude all mastery.'[27] In this sense, irony operates

---

[22] Waldrop, *Lawn of Excluded Middle*, p.31.
[23] ibid, p.68.
[24] ibid, p.18.
[25] ibid, p.13.
[26] Paul de Man, 'The Rhetoric of Temporality, *Blindness and Insight: Essays in the Rhetoric of Contemporary Criticism* (London: Methuen, 1983) p.211.
[27] Blanchot, *The Writing of the Disaster*, p.35.

as a kind of interference. In other words, as with the hermeneutic principle of *Mahloket*, but also in a manner reminiscent of the work of translation, irony is always *in other words*. Thus irony's tools of paraphrase, partial quotation, misquotation, approximation, analogy, association, misidentification, pastiche, parody, are not signs of critical inefficiency but rather reflect all the more fully the non-coincidence or difference of the literary work from itself.

In the closing section of *Otherwise than Being or, Beyond Essence*, Emmanuel Levinas outlines a similar argument in the context of scepticism. Scepticism, Levinas argues, is a form of argument that takes place as the cancellation of its own expression. Scepticism prohibits comprehension, Levinas argues, because the equivocation it names inevitably puts all deductive reasoning into question. In Levinas' terms, scepticism:

> traverses the rationality or logic of knowledge [and] is a refusal to synchronize the implicit affirmation contained in saying and the negation which this affirmation states in the said.[28]

As such, scepticism produces no form of counter-knowledge, which is to say, it does not produce a *veritas* of refutation. Scepticism is always double, both 'without end and without continuity.'[29] As a result, Levinas goes on to claim that the discourse of scepticism points to a language that would:

> exceed the limits of what is thought, by suggesting, letting be understood without ever making understandable, an implication of a meaning distinct from that which comes to signs from the simultaneity of systems or the logical definition of concepts.[30]

In so doing, scepticism opens towards a thought of language indivisible from its crossings and traversal. Scepticism requires that language be counter-positional, that it proceed in fits and starts, with questions and effacements, in a manner always turning, always wandering against the limit of what it has not been quite possible to say, always forming, always falling.

---

[28] Emmanuel Levinas, *Otherwise than Being or, Beyond Essence*, trans. Alphonso Lingis (Dordrecht: Kluwer Academic Publishers, 1991) p.167.
[29] Levinas, *Otherwise than Being*, p.169.
[30] ibid, pp.169-170.

Equally, the non-specifiable emptiness at the centre ('the center of nothing') of Waldrop's sequence calls any claims that work makes into question.[31] In the absence of self-identical signs what forms into legibility across the poem is not so much the negation of signification as the plenitude of a between-space marked by perpetual linguistic non-coincidence. From this perspective, the literal sense of alterity as 'change' or 'alteration' necessarily underwrites presence and absence with an incommensurable opening. The consequence of such constant shifting is that 'the I has no sharp boundary inward' or outward but simply a perpetual sense of lack or 'inability.'[32] The lawn of excluded middle becomes a place where language fails or, perhaps more properly, 'breaks free' such that it might be thought of along the lines of an event horizon, as outlined by general relativity, namely as a boundary beyond which no event can be observed.

'We must force ourselves open to discoveries across the grain, contrary to what we comfortably know,' writes the American poet, Forrest Gander. 'In this we may be led best by silence, [a] gesture of openness.'[33] It is hard to know what words might best describe such a language, how they might shepherd a body to the page and spell life. Order is everything. Gesture is a fragile art made of many pieces, the majority of which go unnoticed; it is what Stefan Brecht, in another context, has called a 'non-verbal, arational communication,' an interlinear interchange.[34] Writing slips from immaterial sign to physical surface; it screens a spacing of graphemes that except phonemics, that turn inside out the common structures of equivalence and of reference. It is 'something that can be held in the mouth, deeply, like darkness', that can be experienced as material sensation but which 'goes by so fast when I should like to see it laid open to view [...] so that form becomes its own explanation.'[35] The pages turn and the typeset separation of the poem becomes nothing more than 'the thickness silence gains when pressed,' letter pressed.[36] 'The ghosts of grammar veer toward shape' and disperse there just as 'touching bottom means the water's over your

---

[31] Waldrop, *Lawn of Excluded Middle*, p.13.
[32] Waldrop, *Split Infinites*, p.54.
[33] Forrest Gander, *A Faithful Existence*, p.17.
[34] Stefan Brecht, *The Original Theatre of the City of New York: From the Mid 60s to the Mid 70s*, Book 1, *The Theatre of Visions: Robert Wilson* (Frankfurt: Suhrkamp Verlag, 1978) p.278.
[35] Waldrop, *Lawn of Excluded Middle*, pp.6 and 10.
[36] ibid, p.17.

head. And you can't annul a shake of that by shaking it again.'[37]

In spite of all this, however, it is important to stress that this conceptual and structural shadow-zone paradoxically both manifests and fosters alterity, in the sense that the poem's semantic sliding appears not only as but, crucially, because of the error of writing. 'Only language grows such grass-green grass' Waldrop writes in the third section of *Lawn of Excluded Middle,* by which she means only language extrapolates the *lawn* of excluded middle, the hollow space it both contains and names.[38] Language reflects the empty centre by signing that which goes astray, namely, narrative, grammar, syntax, sequence. Indeed, when Waldrop writes that 'sincerity is no help once we admit to the lies we tell on nocturnal occasions' the point is that, because language can be used to lie, to say *anything,* it can never be mobilised as a vehicle for certainty.[39] There is a word too many. In order to get at language, therefore, it is necessary to accentuate what undercuts it, 'to cultivate the gap itself with its high grass for privacy and reference gone astray.'[40] The lawn, in this sense, becomes 'the locus of fertility,'[41] 'scrap meanings amplifying the succession of green perspectives, moist features, spasms on the lips.'[42]

It is no coincidence that Waldrop's language is inflected by an implicit feminist discourse. Throughout *Lawn of Excluded Middle* the female body is imagined as one of the exemplary expressions of the 'excluded middle'. As Waldrop writes unequivocally in the notes that append the sequence, the excluded middle is 'the womb, the empty center of the woman's body.'[43] This idea develops part of the scope of her earlier volume, *The Reproduction of Profiles,* which worked to problematize logical syntax by sliding different frames of reference together. Indeed, the similarity of project was made even more apparent when these volumes were later collected as the first and second parts of the 2006 trilogy, *Curves to the Apple,* with *Reluctant Gravities* concluding the sequence. As Waldrop explains, on one level at least the work collected in *Curves to the Apple* 'especially brings in the female

---

[37] ibid, pp.17 and 20.
[38] ibid, p.8.
[39] ibid, p.17.
[40] ibid, p.17.
[41] ibid, p.68. Waldrop repeats this description of *Lawn of Excluded Middle* in *Ceci,* p.91.
[42] ibid, p.17.
[43] ibid, p.68.

body and sets into play the old gender archetypes of logic and mind being "male," whereas "female" designates the illogical: emotion, body, matter.' 'I hope,' Waldrop adds, 'that the constant sliding challenges these categories.'[44] Various critics have developed this aspect of Waldrop's poetics, Kimberley Lamm noting how 'Waldrop uses the malleable language and imaginaries of poetry to wrestle the feminine away from its insertion into these gaps and exposes the strange configurations of materials, concepts, and desires whirling away within them.'[45] For Waldrop, the key is to challenge these categories and classifications in order to demonstrate the ways in which such classifications are false constructs. For Waldrop it is not so much a case of opposing the feminine to the masculine as emphasising the more indistinguishable zone in which these categorisations fall to pieces. As Waldrop comments in interview, 'writing is beyond gender distinctions.' As she goes on to add, to her mind writing 'would be androgynous, would partake of both male and female modes of thinking.'[46] 'Every writer,' Waldrop writes elsewhere, 'is androgyne. Imaginative writing is inclusive.'[47]

This is why, in interview, Waldrop is keen to emphasise the ways in which the empty centre is the necessary space that, in its inability, enables 'resonance, understanding, fertility, everything. This is where the "law" (of the "excluded middle") turns into "lawn."'[48] To put it another way, it is where the 'law' is at once both legislated (written) and suspended by its exception. The exception puts the law into question, but it also structures that law as the play of this intractable question. Here the question of the law, or better, the law as question, is what grows on the lawn of excluded middle, what blurs into focus, 'the way words rally to the blanks between them and thus augment the volume of

---

[44] Waldrop, 'Alarms and Excursions,' *Dissonance*, p.178.
[45] Kimberley Lamm, 'Ceci n'est pas Keith / Ceci n'est pas Rosmarie: Writing Another Language for Feminist Poetics,' in *Another Language: Poetic Experiments in Britain and North America* (Münster, Lit Verlag, 2008), p.263 [pp.263-273]. See also, Kimberley Lamm's 'Gender in a Minor Key: Rosmarie Waldrop's *A Key into the Language of America*,' and Deborah Meadows, 'Rosmarie Waldrop and Poetics of Embodied Philosophy,' both in *How2*, Vol.1, No. 8 (Fall, 2002), http://www.asu.edu/pipercwcenter/how2journal/archive/online_archive/v1_8_2002/current/readings/index-waldrop.htm, accessed 12 July 2012.
[46] Retallack, 'A Conversation with Rosmarie Waldrop,' p.361.
[47] Waldrop, *Lavish Absence*, p.51.
[48] Retallack, 'A Conversation with Rosmarie Waldrop,' p.365.

their resonance.'[49] As section twenty-two puts it: 'in language nothing is hidden or our own, its light indifferent to holes in the present or postulates beginning with ourselves.'[50] 'Caught between simulation and paradox' language gives 'everything' precisely because, in its turnings, it casts any definitive assertion from Derrida's *différance*, that radical play of difference and deferral.[51]

The consequence of such difference is that the space of language, or what Waldrop, quoting Keats, would refer to as 'negative capability,'[52] gives rise only to the non-voice of the neuter, 'this Excluded Middle [...] [t]he anonymous and incessant droning [...] at once affirmative and negative,'[53] where possibilities and contradictions are 'held in balance.'[54] This is why Blanchot defines the neuter as 'that which cannot be assigned to any genre whatsoever: the non-general, the non-generic, as well as the non-particular.'[55] The excluded middle is strictly anonymous; it is that which:

> pronounces itself without there being a position or deposition of existence, without presence or absence affirming it, without the unity of the word coming to dislodge it from the between-the-two in which it disseminates itself.[56]

In Waldrop, it is this condition of being always elsewhere and always already separate, even from itself, that determines the excluded middle as the 'nowhere' of an empty centre that both swells and suspends each word and expression. Because the excluded middle is exceptional rather than positional, the excluded middle effectively strips both language and itself of any precise point of reference. Read this way, the excluded middle is at once a double movement and a double bind. It doubles

---

[49] Waldrop, *Lawn of Excluded Middle*, p.11.
[50] ibid, p.27.
[51] ibid, p.24.
[52] In a letter, Keats writes: '*Negative Capability*, that is when man is capable of being in uncertainties, Mysteries, doubts, without any irritable reaching after fact and reason.' John Keats, Letter to George and Tom Keats, 21, 27? Dec. 1817; quoted in Waldrop, *Lavish Absence*, p.83.
[53] Emmanuel Levinas, 'A Conversation with André Dalmas,' *Proper Names*, trans. Michael B. Smith (Stanford, CA: Stanford University Press, 1996) p.152.
[54] Waldrop, 'The Ground is the Only Figure,' p.238.
[55] Blanchot, *The Infinite Conversation*, p.299.
[56] Maurice Blanchot, *The Step Not Beyond*, trans. Lycette Nelson (Albany, NY: State University of New York Press, 1992) p.35.

back in the instant of conceptualisation insofar as all that remains is the outline trace of its non-recognition dispersing across an irreducible distance. As a result, the excluded middle is little more than the relation with the unknown, the primordial 'saying' of language, Waldrop's 'spasms on the lips' that do not so much spew words as stammer a sense, vague and just a little sceptical, of the shadow-zone. Everything depends on the noun not there, blurred into the margins of text, the texture of paper, the spacing of letters.

Another Language

In various essays, interviews, and texts Waldrop gathers together these various inflections of the empty centre under the sign of 'God'. As Waldrop puts it in 'The Ground is the Only Figure':

> God as void, infinite, nothingness, silence, death, desert. As ultimate otherness. As metaphor for all that calls us into question. Our primal opponent. The center we long for, which, we think, would give meaning to our lives [...] but that remains unreachable.[1]

For Waldrop, the name of 'God' is the mark of a question, the space towards which the mind travels and into which language disappears. As Bataille writes:

> God is nothing if He is not, in every sense, the surpassing of God [...] We cannot with impunity incorporate the very word into our speech which surpasses words, the word *God*; directly we do so, this word, surpassing itself, explodes past its defining, restrictive limits. That which this word is, stops nowhere, is checked by nothing, it is everything and, everywhere, is impossible to overtake anywhere.[2]

To put it another way, the encounter (intellectual, physical, spiritual) with the infinite throws us away from ourselves, outside ourselves, outside frames of reference and known coordinates. It is a process of exposure and there are no words for such an experience except those that except themselves, that stumble, falter, know no course and cast boundlessness; 'allowing ourselves to be lost, we dive into the infinite of language.'[3]

The influence of Jabès weighs heavy here, Jabès' sense of God as metaphor, as 'shorthand for what we find as we try to know ourselves, as we test our limits and try to think the unthinkable, know the unknowable' and come into contact with what Waldrop terms 'a vertigo

---

[1] Waldrop, 'The Ground is the Only Figure,' p.250.
[2] Georges Bataille, *Madame Edwarda*, in *My Mother, Madame Edwarda, The Dead Man*, trans. Austryn Wainhouse (London and New York: Marion Boyars, 1995) p.142.
[3] Waldrop, 'Split Infinite,' p.186.

of selves.'[4] 'God' as shorthand, a cleft, a cleaving:

> Narrow rooms. When we say infinite we have no conception but our own inability. Therefore the name God is used. The I has no sharp boundaries inward.[5]

For Waldrop the question of the empty middle matters because it marshals a space of the question, the proximity, she argues, following Jabès, between truth and vertigo: *verité* and *vertige*.[6] Crucially, the point is that such proximity negates the sedentary, the fixed, the certain. Everything is on the move and any ground is only temporary. As Maurice Blanchot knew so well: the most profound question is the one that has yet to be asked.[7] So it is, Waldrop comments, 'the relations between the terms keep shifting. No one metaphor is central or even more important than another.' Rather, as she continues:

> In the end we are left with gestures: the gesture of analogy rather than any particular analogy, the gesture of signification rather than any particular meaning, the gestures of endless commentary and interpretation. A wild whirl to cover the abyss. Vertigo. Our gestures, too, are empty. But they have a resonance that grows out of the consent to emptiness. As do instruments. As does language, depending on the blank space that is the matter between words, that allows them to be.[8]

From this perspective, what Waldrop's material and linguistic thematisation of the excluded middle demands is the spacing of another language, which would be featureless, androgynous, without property and without propriety. 'Language, in its full range,' Waldrop writes, 'is other.'[9] In many senses, such a new or otherwise language would be one of dislocation, a foreign tongue cleaving words that 'vanish[...] into communication' in order that the roof of the mouth might speak behind them, in their dissipating folds,[10] 'the same way deeper meaning

---

[4] ibid, pp.183 and 185.
[5] ibid, p.54.
[6] ibid, p.184.
[7] Maurice Blanchot, 'The Most Profound Question,' *The Infinite Conversation*, pp.11-24.
[8] Waldrop, 'Split Infinite,' p.185.
[9] Waldrop, 'Thinking of Follows,' p.208.
[10] Waldrop, *Lawn of Excluded Middle*, p.61.

may constrict a sentence right out of the language into an uneasiness.'[11] What is ultimately at stake in the excluded middle is a form of language (and, by extension, a mode of being-in-the-world) that does not authorise itself under the declaratory sign of self-control but rather that indicates itself in the event of its own rupture. Nothing specific happens because of the excluded middle. It does not produce anything, quantifiable or otherwise; or, better, it produces nothing other than the error of misidentification and mispronunciation, the word that sticks in the mouth's cavity. In the screen of its sliding surface, the concern of the excluded middle is a concern for what remains when the sovereignty of self-possession (of being, of language) escapes. It is about trying to get out, not so much in order to get into anything else, but simply to get out and to stay in this outside. As Blanchot comments reflectively of Waldrop's notion of the imperative of poetry to 'short-circuit' the regulation of linguistic communication, the precise task of the poet is:

> to call us obstinately back to error, to turn us toward that space where everything we propose, everything we have acquired, everything we are, all that opens upon the earth and in the sky, returns to insignificance, and where what approaches is the nonserious and the nontrue, as if perhaps thence sprang the source of all authenticity.[12]

On the one hand, the excluded middle dispossesses the law of meaning from any sovereign guarantee. On the other hand, this lack impels language to err repeatedly, to breakdown, to fragment, and thus, according to both Waldrop and Blanchot, to release the truth of language, that is, its non-truth, the truth of another language that neither arrives nor stills. Another language is a language of counter-rhythm, nameless and detaching, that speaks both as and in the interruption of speech, as and in the lightening of language's between-point. It is a turning inside out, a sequence of corridors whose 'distance doesn't seem to lessen no matter how straight [the] course.'[13]

Waldrop exemplifies this sense of double movement here when she writes that it is:

> [a]s if I had to navigate both forward and backward, part of me turned away from where I'm going, taking the distance of long

---

[11] ibid, p.27.
[12] Blanchot, *The Space of Literature*, p.247, n. 8.
[13] Waldrop, *Lawn of Excluded Middle*, p.30.

corridors to allow for delay and trouble, for keeping in the dark while being led on.[14]

In his 1721 essay, 'De Motu', Bishop George Berkeley claimed that 'the physicist studies the series or successions of sensible things, noting by what laws they are connected, and in what order, what precedes as cause, and what follows as effect.'[15] As Philonous tells Hylas, 'the more a man knows of the connexion of ideas, the more he is said to know of the nature of things.'[16] Throughout that essay, Berkeley contends that notions of absolute space and time are, in themselves, without meaning. For Berkeley only sense experience may underwrite meaning. Since neither space nor time has any foundation in sense experience, Berkeley argues, there is no reason to accept them as meaningful words. Rather, Berkeley develops the notion that all empirical signification is entirely conditional on effects. Writing nearly two hundred years later, Ernst Mach remarked how 'the intuition of space is bound up with the organisation of the senses [...] We are not justified,' Mach goes on, 'in ascribing spatial properties to things which are not perceived by the senses.'[17] Similarly, theories of metric expansion suggest the opening out of the universe is intrinsic: it is defined, simply, as the relative separation of its own parts rather than any motion outward into something else. It is also possible for a distance to exceed the speed of light multiplied by the age of the universe, which means that light from one part of space might still be arriving at distant locations. As the universe expands and the scale of what is observable contracts, the distance to the edge of what can be seen gets closer and closer. While this may sound potentially instructive, when the edge of what is observable becomes smaller than a body, gravitation is unbound and falling away becomes scattering.

The 'shadow-zone' that interrupts language, that turns away even as this turning is also to be understood as a leading, lets through the texture of another language, but one that is always already blotted, that has spread outwards to the margins of the page, disappearing there at the letter's edge. Strictly speaking, for Waldrop, another language is neither discursive nor communicable but simply a blanking into

---

[14] ibid, p.36.
[15] Bishop George Berkeley, 'De Motu,' *The Works of George Berkeley, Bishop of Cloyne*, eds. A. Luce and T. Jessop (London: Thomas Nelson, 1951), Vol. 4, p.51.
[16] Berkeley, *The Works of George Berkeley*, Vol. 2, p.245.
[17] Ernst Mach, *The Conservation of Energy* (La Salle, IL: Open Court, 1911) pp.91 and 87.

ink without correlate or correspondence. As Waldrop writes, 'the ink washes into a deeper language, and in the end the water runs clear.'[18] Here, another language hangs suspended, on the edge of forming, on the edge of falling.

In interview Werner Heisenberg talked about the ways in which the new physics required a similarly new conception of language, one that registered uncertainty by rendering the seemingly precise language of science equivocal. Heisenberg's comment is instructive of the general point involved here:

> The point is we are bound up with a language, we are hanging in the language. If we want to do physics, we must describe our experiments and the results to other physicists, so that they can be verified or checked by others. At the same time, we know that the words we use to describe the experiments have only a limited range of applicability. That is a fundamental paradox which we have to confront. We cannot avoid it; we have simply to cope with it, to find what is the best thing we can do about it.[19]

Despite numerous attempts, the question of how to modify language, to allow reverberations and murmurs, the space of doubt, blank territories, remains a question. 'I use vocabulary from the new physics', Waldrop writes, 'because it is the discipline that seems to have the most negative capability at this point,'[20] with Waldrop going on to specify 'the paradox of quantum and wave, in the simultaneous presence of fragment and flow.'[21]

In *Lavish Absence* Waldrop counter-threads fact with vertigo, suggesting vertigo as a precarious ground from which to approach notions of knowledge and understanding and life and relation:

> Vertigo. The terms shift. The relation of the terms shifts. The richness undermines itself. If everything is like something else, no one likeness means anything [...] we are left with 'pure' analogy, the *gesture* of it rather than any one specific analogy. A gesture that makes the terms transparent for the very structure

---

[18] Waldrop, *Lawn of Excluded Middle*, p.36.
[19] Werner Heisenberg, quoted in Paul Buckley and F. David Peat, *Glimpsing Reality: Ideas in Physics and the Link to Biology* (Toronto: University of Toronto Press, 1996) p.7.
[20] Retallack, 'A Conversation with Rosmarie Waldrop,' p.363.
[21] ibid, p.373-4.

of language, of signification [...] Transparency for the structure of signification—and for its limits: the silence, the infinite, the nothing, all it is not able to hold.[22]

As a point of departure, as a standing outside, such a powerless speech is a coming back to the surface-grain of a page that writing both projects and veils. 'I think,' Waldrop writes, 'on paper,'[23] in 'lines that carry the weight of absence,'[24] and where 'the difference of shadow bespeaks other crossroads.'[25]

As Blanchot writes, 'to live with the unknown before one (which also means: to live before the unknown, and before oneself as unknown) is to enter into the responsibility of a speech that speaks without exercising any form of power.'[26] A poetics of another language works by indirection, in side-step, yet what it affects is the motivation toward reservation, toward a quiet holding back, a swelling of the irreducible measure of distance. Among other things, this other language is an 'element of structure' that spreads out and scatters. It has this dispersal as its precondition. It is other ways leaking into filament; a scurrying sideways of signification; diffraction, deflection. On the edge of writing, it stammers and chinks a present tense for reference.

---

[22] Waldrop, *Lavish Absence*, p.96.
[23] Waldrop, 'Thinking of Follows,' p.213.
[24] Waldrop, *Blindsight*, p.38.
[25] Waldrop. *Ceci*, p.93.
[26] Blanchot, 'René Char and the Thought of the Neutral,' *The Infinite Conversation*, p.302.

Theories of Translation

Waldrop begins the 'Translation' section of her volume of collected essays, *Dissonance*, with an epigraph drawn from Anne Carson which reads, 'the space between two languages is a space like no other.'[1] The translator of over 40 works from French and German, it is this 'no other' which is particularly relevant to understanding Waldrop's theory and practice of translation. For Waldrop, that is, translation is non-equivalent. In a manner similar to her determination of the space of the between, for Waldrop translation does not aim at the simple transmission of content, but rather opens a rift between word and meaning, a discord which, in its opening, draws attention to a strangeness at the heart of language, a restlessness which does something else, something other than simply render a work from one language to another. As Edwin Gentlzer points out, etymologically 'translate' is derived from the Latin word *translatus*, meaning 'carried over', and *translatus* is the past participle of *transferre*, whereby:

> the Latin *ferre* means 'to carry' or 'to transport' as in carrying a shield, and was often used to mean to bear or convey with the notion of motion (Homer), as in ships borne by the forces of wind. It also meant to endure, to suffer, as in to bear a mental burden, and survives in expressions such as 'you're not faring well' [...] translation refers to the sense of roads or ways that lead to a place, as in a door leading to a garden, or a road leading to a city, conveying a sense of stretching or extension toward.[2]

In her essay from 1984, 'The Joy of the Demiurge', Waldrop wonders about the reasons for engaging so fully in such an activity. 'I have often asked myself why I go on translating,' Waldrop comments, 'instead of concentrating exclusively on writing my own poetry. The woes of the translator are all too well known: little thanks, poor pay, and plenty of abuse.'[3] Add to this, Waldrop continues, the reluctance of American publishers to include non-commissioned translations in their catalogues, and the sheer persistence of Waldrop's enterprise seems

---

[1] Waldrop, 'Translation,' *Dissonance*, p.135.
[2] Edwin Gentzler, *Contemporary Translation Theories* (Clevedon: Multilingual Matters, 2001) p.166.
[3] Waldrop, 'The Joy of the Demiurge,' *Dissonance*, p.137

Theories of Translation 117

perhaps even more idiosyncratic. Occasionally, Waldrop writes, the process and discipline of translation has helped refocus her own writing when it had stalled. Similarly, at least in part her interest in translation stems from an interest in assuming the role of 'mediator' between languages, although as Waldrop also adds, if that really was one of the central motivations behind her work as a translator, she would have served readers better simply by 'teaching them the language.'[4] Perhaps unsurprisingly, Waldrop also suggests her own personal circumstances as a German-born poet with American citizenship writing in a second language and living in and between two spaces as potential cause and spur for her ongoing translation work. As Waldrop puts it, 'as an immigrant to the United States, I came to a point where I could not go on writing poems in German while "living" in English. Translating (from English to German, at that time) was the natural substitute.'[5] Yet as Waldrop goes on to add, writing in her adopted language of English 'came before translating into it, so that even my particular state as a person between languages cannot altogether account for any persistence in this seemingly unrewarding, nearly impossible activity.'[6]

As might be expected from these comments, Waldrop locates the main reasons for her continued engagement in the work of translation somewhere else, that elusive other world of the elsewhere which, as it turns out, always somehow manages to evade both definition and appropriation, and which carries with it the unsettling yet not uncommon reverberations of the uncanny. 'As I read the original work,' Waldrop writes:

> I admire it. I am overwhelmed. I would like to have written it. Clearly, I am envious—envious enough to make it mine at all cost, at the cost of destroying it. Worse, I take pleasure in destroying the work exactly because it means making it mine. And I assuage what guilt I might feel by promising that I will make reparation, that I will labor to restore the destroyed beauty in my language—also, of course, by the knowledge that *I do not actually touch the original within its own language.*[7]

---

[4] ibid, p.137.
[5] ibid, p.137.
[6] ibid, p.137.
[7] ibid, p.138.

Like every reader, the translator reads through their own experience. As Alberto Manguel puts it, 'beyond the literal sense and the literary meaning, the text we read acquires the projection of our own experience, the shadow, as it were, of who we are.'[8] It is a view that is widespread across translation studies. Christopher Middleton, for instance, himself published by Burning Deck in 1970, echoes this notion of the importance of engagement between translator and the work, commenting in interview how 'it is necessary to know as much as you can about the whole work of the author. Not necessarily about his life and epoch, but to be receptive to the stratagems of his mind, his kind of sentence, and the kind of syntactical behaviour his language shows.'[9] Even in the context of such theories of translation, however, Waldrop's last statement here is striking in its sense of translation as leaving the original work well alone.

For John Johnston such a view corresponds to a sense of translation as a simulacrum. In this regard, and in contradistinction of the Platonic model that privileges similitude and self-identity and construes the simulacrum as negative in respect of its difference to the Idea, the simulacrum is that which simultaneously produces and maintains difference, which de-centres and diverges, and as such opens out into other resonances. Rather than faithfully reproducing meanings of a text, then, Johnston argues translations 'forge a new language, in which both languages are present as two diverging but resonant series of words. In a reversal of the relationship between "original" and "imitation," the translations propose themselves as the "origin" of a new set of meanings sometimes indistinguishable from a-signifying verbal intensities.'[10] In this sense, translation does not so much alter the original work as simultaneously preserve its language and recast it into something else, something beyond resemblance. As Johnston continues:

> those translations which accomplish something different by maintaining the originary difference in and through translation, that deterritorialize the target language in such a way that it can't be recoded and recuperated by appeal to

---

[8] Alberto Manguel, *A History of Reading* (London: HarperCollins, 1996) p.267.
[9] Edwin Honig, 'A Conversation with Christopher Middleton,' *MLN*, Vol. 91. No.6 (December 1976) p.1592 (pp.1588-1602).
[10] John Johnston, 'Translation as Simulacrum' in Lawrence Venuti (ed.), *Rethinking Translation: Discourse, Subjectivity, Ideology* (London: Routledge, 1992) p.49.

established cultural and spiritual meanings, that thereby manifest something new in the language, are also simulacra, diverging from the original but also resonant with it, bringing to fulfilment or pushing along further what the original carried only as a precursor.[11]

It is precisely the implications of such an argument that underpins Waldrop's notion of translation as what she terms 'irreducible strangeness'. For Waldrop, translation is an act of exploration, a 'double exploration', because 'the translator must not only explore the original, but also search the target language for an idiom, a language within language.'[12] As Walter Benjamin writes in his essay, 'The Task of the Translator,' translation should aim to 'expand and deepen [...] language by means of the foreign language,' to sound 'some strangeness in the proportion', 'a trace of the foreign in the translation.'[13] For Benjamin, that is to say, the 'transmission' or 'carrying of one to another' of translation is centred on notions of contiguity rather than similitude. Every translator, Benjamin suggests, 'lives by the difference of languages; every translation is founded upon this difference.'[14] As a consequence, it is not so much that a translation seeks to resemble the work to be translated, but rather, as Blanchot notes, that translation raises 'a question of an identity on the basis of alterity: the same work in two languages, both because of their foreignness and by making visible, in their foreignness, what makes this work such that it will always be *other*.'[15] The translated work, in other words, is never at home.[16]

As a result of this alterity, Benjamin continues, 'translation must in large measure refrain from wanting to communicate something, from rendering the sense.'[17] Here Benjamin echoes the hugely influential ideas on translation set out by the German Romantic Friedrich Schleiermacher's concept of 'foreignisation' and of bringing the reader

---

[11] Johnston, 'Translation as Simulacrum,' p.54.
[12] Waldrop, *Lavish Absence*, p.7.
[13] Walter Benjamin, 'The Task of the Translator,' in *Illuminations: Essays and Reflections*, ed. Hannah Arendt (New York: Schoken Books, 1968), p.74. See also, Waldrop, 'The Joy of the Demiurge,' p.140.
[14] Maurice Blanchot, 'Translating,' *Friendship*, p.58.
[15] ibid, pp.59-60.
[16] For more on the 'unhomeliness' of translation, see Andrew Benjamin, 'Translating Origins: Psychoanalysis and Philosophy,' in Lawrence Venuti (ed.), *Rethinking Translation*, pp.18-41.
[17] Walter Benjamin, 'The Task of the Translator,' p.81.

to the foreign text, that is, of aiming 'to give the reader, through the translation, the impression he would have received as a German reading the work in the original language.'[18] Or as Wilhelm von Humboldt put it a year later in his introduction to his translation of Aeschylus' *Agamemnon* in 1816, it is important to give 'the translation a certain tinge of foreignness.'[19] Yet while one of Benjamin's main critical aims was to conceive a practice of translation which does not attempt to sound as if it were written in the host language, Benjamin's ultimate and increasingly influential hermeneutic notion of 'translatability' or 'pure language' marks the point at which Benjamin's and Waldrop's conceptions of translation diverge most significantly. For Benjamin, that is to say, translation aims both for a kind of illumination and liberation, one currently forgotten but which precedes the attempt to build the tower of Babel when, according to the Book of Genesis, the whole earth was of one language, and of one speech and which the Kabbalists believed was also the language of paradise. 'Seen thus,' George Steiner writes, 'translation is a teleological imperative, a stubborn searching out of all the apertures, translucencies, sluice-gates through which the divided streams of human speech pursue their destined return to a single sea.'[20]

Yet it is a form of illumination and liberation that also remains faithful to Saint Paul's excursus on *pneuma* in I Corinthians 14. There, Paul emphasises an irresolvable differentiation between letter and spirit that prohibits the translation of 'spirit', 'authentic speech', and that understands the words of Christ to be beyond the scope of human discourse, as that which is unspeakable. In an interesting echo of the above sense of foreignisation, for Paul this constitutes an 'arcana verba', a language of tongues, inassimilable, always already non-equivalent, foreign, otherwise, those noumena which, in Kant's phrase, 'mark the limits of our sensible knowledge' and which 'leave open a space which we can fill neither through possible experience nor through pure understanding.'[21] Translation, St Paul goes on to elucidate in II

---

[18] Friedrich Schleiermacher, 'On the Different Methods of Translating' in Lawrence Venuti (ed.), *The Translation Studies Reader* (London: Routledge, 2004) p.50.
[19] Wilhem von Humboldt, 'The More Faithful, the More Divergent,' in Douglas Robinson, *Western Translation Theory: From Herodotus to Nietzsche* (Manchester: St Jerome Publishing, 1997) p.240.
[20] George Steiner, *After Babel: Aspects of Language and Translation* (London: Oxford University Press, 1975) p.244.
[21] Immanuel Kant, *Critique of Pure Reason*, trans. Norman Kemp Smith

Corinthians 12:4, would be blasphemy, or at the very least that form of translation which does not simultaneously erase itself in the face of its tracing of the foreign, translating the untranslatable *as untranslatable*. As Christopher Middleton puts it, 'one of the simplest and most creative ways of considering the act of translation is to regard it as a minimal, perhaps vestigial, but still exemplary encounter with "the other."'[22] Translation is exemplary precisely because it registers difference *qua* difference, because it is not quite equivalent, because it leaves a space open for disagreement and disappearance, Heraclitus' one differing in itself, *hen diapheron heautoi*, where *diapherein* is based on the root *diaphero* which means 'to carry from one to the other, to carry across,' but which in Heraclitus also carries the metaphorical meaning 'to toss about, to be disrupted' and which Derrida, in *Margins of Difference*, goes on to term the 'play of traces' or *différance*.[23] The absent text, Middleton continues, 'is the one we are helped to conceive of by the existence of the text before us.'[24] Or as Forrest Gander puts it, 'in a good translation, the original may be veiled, but it doesn't disappear.'[25] Walter Benjamin: good translation does 'not cover the original, does not block its light, but allows the pure language, as though reinforced by its own medium, to shine upon the original all the more fully.'[26]

Waldrop's reading of Benjamin's sense of 'pure language' is both more pragmatic and more material. For Waldrop, in other words, 'pure language' is an abstraction premised first and foremost on the assumption of a 'central relationship between languages', the possibility of which is confirmed by the fact that translation is considered possible at all.[27] Waldrop's critical difference here stems from her sense that translation does not progress towards some kind of abstraction but, on the contrary, 'toward another embodiment in a concrete, particular language.'[28] In this, Waldrop suggests, the task of the translator is not to try to render the original work *as it is* in another language but

---

(Basingstoke and New York: Palgrave, 1929) p.A289/B343.
[22] Honig, 'A Conversation with Christopher Middleton,' p.1596.
[23] Jacques Derrida, *Margins of Philosophy*, trans. Alan Bass (Chicago and London: University of Chicago Press, 1982) p.15. See also: Henry George Liddell and Robert Scott (eds.), *A Greek-English Lexicon* (Oxford: Clarendon, 1925) p.417.
[24] Honig, 'A Conversation with Christopher Middleton,' p.1602.
[25] Forrest Gander, *A Faithful Existence*, p.88.
[26] Benjamin, 'The Task of the Translator,' p.72.
[27] Waldrop, 'The Joy of the Demiurge,' 139.
[28] ibid, 139.

to approximate its '"figures" of thought', in Cicero's famous phrase, Nietzsche's 'movement of style', to give some kind of sense of its form, its rhythm, its tonal structure, its grammar and its contexts, all the while emphasising both the failure of equivalence and the establishment of something, if not new, then different.[29] As Ezra Pound put it when introducing his translations of Cavalcanti, 'it is conceivable the poetry of a far-off time or place requires a translation not only of word and of spirit, but of "accompaniment."'[30] As Waldrop continues, the notion of translation as accompaniment holds also for contemporary works. 'We must understand,' Waldrop writes, 'what Walter Benjamin has described as the intentionality of a work, the ways in which it relates to its language and culture.'[31]

> Translation is approximation rather than duplication. A re-giving of form. I've sometimes described it as trying to get down to the genetic code of a work [...] And from that 'genetic code,' you rebuild it in the other language, but having the instructions that a code would have.[32]

Translations 'are woven into a textual history that is always transforming terms, translating other terms.'[33]

Waldrop here is close to Derrida's recasting of Benjamin's abstracted sense of translation from 'pure language' to the constantly turning, detouring turn of phrase, *différance*.[34] As a result, and in a manner similar to that which underpins her sense of the book rather than the individual poem or line as the primary compositional measure, Waldrop writes how 'the *unit* of translation is the whole work rather than the single sentence or line—let alone the single word.'[35] Waldrop's choice of language underscores her sense of translation as something which, while being related to the original work, is also particular, distinctive,

---

[29] Cicero, *De inventione, De optimo genere oratorum, topica*, trans. H.M. Hubbell (Cambridge, MA: Harvard University Press. 1960) p.364.
[30] Ezra Pound, *Pound's Cavalcanti*, ed. David Anderson (Princeton, NJ: Princeton University Press, 1983) p.12.
[31] Waldrop, *Lavish Absence*, p.55.
[32] Edward Foster, 'An Interview with Rosmarie Waldrop,' *Postmodern Poetry: The Talisman Interviews* (Hoboken, NJ: Talisman House, 1994) p.149.
[33] Getzler, *Contemporary Translation Theories*, p.171.
[34] See Jacques Derrida, 'Des Tours de Babel' in J.F. Graham (ed.), *Difference in Translation* (Ithaca, NY: Cornell University Press, 1985) pp.165-207.
[35] Waldrop, 'The Joy of the Demiurge,' p.139.

different; it is related yet otherwise, the space of the between. Thus, while agreeing with Benjamin's sense that translation, at its best, 'does not cover the original, does not block its light,'[36] Waldrop specifies how, rather than moving toward the Hegelian abstraction of Benjamin's 'pure language', the translated work undergoes 'something more like erosion. It is weathered by the passage of time.'[37] 'A translation that can suggest the lost beauty of the original,' Waldrop goes on to say, 'is preferable to a smooth replica that pretends to be the original itself.'[38] No translation is transparent; 'even the most faithful of translations will bear the mark of the translator, of her time, of her cultural background,' and the cracks upon which the text rests and depends, into which perhaps translation might itself inevitably, clunkily fall, while not being directly visible, might still be felt, and sometimes even more acutely. As Christopher Middleton puts it, such a view of translation enables you 'to look over the edges of the conventions of your own language.'[39] Indeed, it is precisely from the perspective of this effect that Waldrop comments on the ways in which the locus of translation conjures 'new ground somewhere between the two languages, stretching the border of the target language beyond where it was before.'[40] Or as Vincent Broqua puts it, Waldrop writes 'between languages, in the slit, on the edge or in the "doorway" where one language becomes other.' It is 'in this infinitesimal site,' Broqua continues, that Waldrop plays out the exchange of very particular idioms.[41]

Elsewhere Waldrop goes on to align the irreducibly strange work of translation with Hans-Georg Gadamer's notion of the 'third dimension' of a work of literature, that zone where:

> Nothing that is said has its truth simply in itself, but refers instead backward and forward to what is unsaid. Every assertion is motivated, that is, one can sensibly ask of everything that is said, 'Why do you say that?' And only when what is not said is understood along with what is said is an assertion understandable.

---

[36] Benjamin, 'The Task of the Translator,' p.70.
[37] Waldrop, 'The Joy of the Demiurge,' p.142.
[38] ibid, p.143.
[39] Honig, 'A Conversation with Christopher Middleton,' p.1596.
[40] Waldrop, 'Irreducible Strangeness,' *Dissonance*, p.156.
[41] Vincent Broqua, 'Pressures 'Pressures of Never-at-home,' *Jacket* 32 (April, 2007), http://jacketmagazine/32/p-broqua.shtml,' para. 67; accessed 19 December 2011.

As Waldrop puts it, 'it takes words to make things visible.'[42] Here silence becomes a space 'for the utterance rather than an ultimate limit' and 'a space,' Waldrop writes, no matter how transitive, 'can be explored, even this space of the unsaid.'[43]

Within the contexts of these theoretical perspectives, and following a tradition of translation practice stretching back to Dryden and Goethe but being perhaps developed most significantly in Roman Jakobson's sense of the translation process consisting of the intralingual, the interlingual and the intersemiotic,[44] Waldrop's practice of translation goes through three main stages. The first stage, Waldrop notes, involves an intense period of reading in tandem with an initial and very loose drafting process. As Waldrop puts it, during this process she is not after simply what the work says but rather both an understanding of and engagement with its very creative process, its procedures, methods, and idiosyncrasies, formal or otherwise. In the second stage Waldrop disregards the original entirely, treating what she calls 'the mess of the first draft (which is not quite English, often makes no sense at all) as if it were a draft of my own' and attempts to make a work of her own out of it. Waldrop refers to this stage as 'the stage of separation.'[45] In the third stage, Waldrop returns to the original text and tries to 'wrestle the English as close to the original language as possible.'[46] Often the main work involved in this final stage revolves around syntax and rhythm, around letting the shape and flow of the translation approach those in the original text, around letting the translated work exist in the space of the between, in the space of open form, which however open is still a form, still contains bounds; or as Goethe formulated it, letting it be known that the translated text does not exist 'instead of the other but in its place.'[47] George Steiner, in his hugely influential outline of the history of translation, *After Babel*, argues for the vital and expressive importance of this unresolved space of the between, writing how:

> Good translation [...] can be defined as that in which the dialectic of impenetrability and ingress, of intractable alienness

---

[42] Waldrop, 'Silence, the Devil, and Jabès,' *Dissonance*, p.149.
[43] ibid, pp.150-1.
[44] For a brief overview of Jakobson's theory, see Jeremy Munday, *Introducing Translation Studies: Theories and Applications* (London: Routledge, 2001) pp.37-8.
[45] Waldrop, 'Irreducible Strangeness,' p.159.
[46] ibid, p.158.
[47] Quoted in George Steiner, *After Babel*, p.258.

and felt 'at-homeness' remains unresolved, but expressive. Out of the tension of resistance and affinity, a tension directly proportional to the proximity of the two languages and historical communities, grows the elucidative strangeness of the great translation.[48]

As Waldrop puts it, and as with her poetics more generally, 'translation's ultimate task may be to bear witness to the *essentially* irreducible strangeness between languages – but its immediate task is exactly to explore this space,' the shape of thinking a text makes.[49] In this, Waldrop argues, translation is a process of 'dialogue and collaboration.'[50] Indeed, this is precisely why Maurice Blanchot holds that translation 'is the sheer play of difference: it constantly makes allusion to difference, dissimulates difference, but by occasionally revealing and often accentuating it, translation becomes the very life of this difference.'[51] 'Not resemblance,' Blanchot goes on to develop, 'but identity on the basis of otherness.'[52] '"Otherness,"' Waldrop writes in relation to Jabès, 'is the condition of individuation, the condition of being set apart from the rest of creation in the glorious—and murderous—species of humankind and, in addition, set apart from our fellow humans as individuals, always "other."'[53] Alberto Manguel puts it in the following terms:

> As we read a text in our own language, the text itself becomes a barrier. We can go into it as far as its words allow, embracing all their possible definitions; we can bring other texts to bear upon it and to reflect it, as in a hall of mirrors; we can construct another, critical text that will extend and illuminate the one we are reading; but we cannot escape the fact that its language is the limit of our universe. Translation proposes a sort of parallel universe, another space and time in which the text reveals other, extraordinary possible meanings. For these meanings, however, there are no words, since they exist in the intuitive no man's land between the language of the original and the

---

[48] George Steiner, *After Babel*, p.413.
[49] Waldrop, 'Irreducible Strangeness,' p.159.
[50] Waldrop, *Lavish Absence*, p.63.
[51] Maurice Blanchot, 'Translating,' p.58.
[52] ibid, p.58; also quoted in Waldrop, *Lavish Absence*, p.63.
[53] Waldrop, *Lavish Absence*, p.3.

language of the translator.[54]

When the text that is to be translated is itself already linguistically complex the theoretical and practical problems of translation becomes even more acute. As Forrest Gander asks, 'how are we to deal with an original text that is itself syntactically innovative? If the literal-syntax translator translates a conventional word order (in the original language) into an unconventional order (in the target language), how can work that is unconventional in the first place be given its due?'[55]

---

[54] Manguel, *A History of Reading*, p.276.
[55] Gander, *A Faithful Existence*, p.118.

All Strange Away: Translating Jabès

Given the particular type of innovative work Waldrop usually translates, it is a question which inevitably preoccupies much of Waldrop's practical work as a translator, but perhaps nowhere more acutely than in her landmark translations of Edmond Jabès, on which she has been engaged for four decades and which has also played one of the most pivotal roles in the development of Waldrop's own poetics.

Waldrop first encountered Jabès' work when she and Keith came across a copy of Jabès' early collected poems, *Je bâtis ma demeure*, in a bookshop in Aix-en-Provence in 1957. Returning to Paris in 1966, Waldrop purchased a copy of the recently published first volume of Jabès' monumental *Le Livre des questions*. As Waldrop describes it, 'it was an overwhelming experience for me to read this first volume. It was a *coup de foudre*.'[1] Or as Waldrop puts it, writing four decades later, 'I know Jabès' work has influenced my attitude toward writing. It has made me see writing as questioning, a questioning that involves one's whole life. It has made me think in terms of book rather than single poem, and at the same time in terms of fragments and perspectives rather than "wholes," "totalities."'[2]

By 1969 Waldrop had translated around fifty pages of *The Book of Questions* but had had the project rejected by all twenty of the publishers she had approached on the basis that, while interesting, translations tended to lose money. As a result, Waldrop temporarily shelved the project, deciding instead to concentrate, at least for a time, on her own writing. Yet Waldrop still travelled with a copy of *Le Livre des questions* when she and Keith were to spend the year 1970-71 on fellowship in Paris, taking Jabès' text as a 'back-up project' in case her own work stuttered to take hold. In January 1970 the American poet, George Tysh, organised a series of poetry readings at the Waldrops' apartment, to which the French poet, Claude Royet-Journoud came and noticed a copy of Jabès' *Le Livre des questions* on the bookshelf. The next afternoon, Royet-Journoud brought Jabès to meet Waldrop. As Waldrop recalls, Jabès was a 'slight' figure, 'a deeply lined face, extraordinary blue eyes. Eyes that seem to be moving outward, toward me. Searching. A sense of gentleness, decorum and warmth. I give him what I have translated. A few days later he recognizes himself in the

---

[1] Edward Foster, 'An Interview with Rosmarie Waldrop', p.140.
[2] Email to author, 27 August 2006.

rhythm.'³

This friendship has sustained and deepened Waldrop's encounter with Jabès' highly individual, idiosyncratic work. In point of fact, the matter of Jabès' influence on the development and shape of Waldrop's own poetics is complex, considered, subtle, personal, intuitive, and built up slowly over a long period of study, attention and friendship. Waldrop credits Jabès with pushing her to think in terms of books as poetic unit, as space, ground, vessel within which to work, its layerings, increments, spacings. Indeed, as Waldrop puts it, it is specifically 'Jabès' insistence on the book on the one hand (as the writer's only place, as Mallarmé's "spiritual instrument") and fragmentation on the other, that focuses my own contradictory impulses toward flow and fragment.'⁴

Waldrop learns from Jabès but there is also a natural aesthetic affinity. Of Jabès Waldrop writes in what can equally serve as a statement on Waldrop's own poetic project:

> His aim is not to invert the traditional hierarchy of sense over sound, but to establish parity between them or, rather, to establish a dynamic relation between language and thinking, where the words do not express pre-existing thoughts, but where their physical characteristics are allowed to lead to new thoughts. Once the physical properties and similarities of words have given the impetus, the semantic dimension is allowed full play to probe and develop the implications.⁵

What really stands out from Jabès' project for Waldrop is the way in which Jabès makes transparent 'the structure of language, of signification. He makes us aware of the imaginary line between signifier and signified by constantly crossing it. And the line between symbol and index. So that at the limits of signification language is made to *show* itself.'⁶ Or again:

> Edmond Jabès writes a text over which he claims no authorial power, a text which he claims only to copy, make legible. This is a remarkable claim in itself [...] everything in his work—the shifting voices and perspectives, the breaks of mode, tautologies, alogical sequences and contradictory metaphors, the stress on

---

[3] Waldrop, *Lavish Absence*, p.5.
[4] ibid, p.75.
[5] ibid, p.70.
[6] ibid, p.87; Waldrop's emphasis.

uncertainty (the constant subjunctive) – all combine to subvert the authority we expect in a book. Authority of statement, of closure and linearity, the confidence in a narrative thread, continuity of temporal and causal sequence. And most of all, the authority of the author.[7]

As Shlomith Rimmon-Kenan explains, 'holes or gaps are so central in narrative fiction because the materials the text provides for the reconstruction of a world (or a story) are insufficient for saturation.'[8] But those holes are also the condition of the world itself, its stutter, its ground, its experience. Thus, for Hank Lazer, 'the qualities of exile, of otherness, of removal, of being beside that recur in Jabès' writing have their foundation (in addition to Jabès' personal, biographical experience) in Jewish history and in Kabbalistic interpretation.'[9]

Here the practice of translation, like the art of reading well, involves being out of place, unsure, unsteady; it entails equivocation. It is to set off, to wander, to go looking, but to find myself travelling in circles, further away, elsewhere. In so doing, it necessitates that such reading be counter-intuitive, that it proceed in fits and starts, with questions and effacements, in manners always turning, always bouncing against the limit of what it is has not been quite possible to say: blindsights, pieces. Thus, as Waldrop puts it, 'the spark given off by the edges of the shards, the fragments, is stronger the more abrupt the cut, the more strongly it makes us feel the lack of transition, the more disparate the surrounding texts.'[10]

Waldrop's main aim is to adhere as closely as possible to Jabès' French, to the effects of his linguistic play, his verbal slippages, his use of puns, sound, complexity; she aims to reproduce his syntax, lexicon and typography, which involves trying to come up with comparable effects, such that Jabes' writing twists English into strange new forms. Waldrop wants, she says, to 'write' Jabès in English, 'write *à l'écoute de* Jabès, write listening to his French.'[11] The methodological question at issue here concerns the criteria for determining the basis for a comparison,

---

[7] ibid, pp.142-3.
[8] Shlomith Rimmon-Kenan, *Narrative Fiction* (London: Methuen, 1983) p.127.
[9] Hank Lazer, 'Meeting in the Book: A Review of *Lavish Absence: Recalling and Rereading Edmond Jabès* by Rosmarie Waldrop,' *Jacket* 23 (August 2003) www. http://jacketmagazine.com/23/lazer-waldr.html, accessed 8 November 2011.
[10] Waldrop, *Lavish Absence*, p.21.
[11] ibid, p.27.

and this is a moot point. As Philip Lewis has noted, this is 'the strong, forceful translation that values experimentation, tampers with usage, seeks to match the polyvalencies or pluralivocities or expressive stresses of the original by producing its own.'[12]

As André Lefevere puts it: 'The translator's task is precisely to render the source text, the original author's interpretation of a given theme expressed in a number of variations, accessible to readers not familiar with these variations, by replacing the original author's variation with their equivalents in a different language, time, place, and tradition. Particular emphasis must be given to the fact that the translator has to replace *all* the variations contained in the source text by their equivalents.'[13]

When specific word play is lost in the process of translation, Waldrop prefers to leave the section in French, accompanied by a more literal but less literary translation. It is, Waldrop writes, an 'awkward' solution but as well as illustrating the manner and mode of the original text, it is a solution which has the added advantage of allowing 'difference, foreignness to come to the fore.' It makes us aware, Waldrop writes, 'of the space *between* the languages where translation lives.'[14]

---

[12] Philip Lewis, 'The Measure of Translation Effects,' in Lawrence Venuti, *Rethinking Translation*, p.261.
[13] André Lefevere, *Translating Poetry: Seven Strategies and a Blueprint* (Assen/Amsterdam: Van Gorcum, 1975) p.99.
[14] Waldrop, *Lavish Absence*, p.71.

Shall We Escape Analogy

At the centre of the French poet, Claude Royet-Journoud's first book, *Le Renversement*, is a page which, in its entirety, reads '*échapperons-nous à l'analogie*' [shall we escape analogy].[1] There is no question mark and the rest of the page is blank. In many respects, this line is tantamount to a characteristically oblique statement by Royet-Journoud on the underlying principle of his own poetics. Royet-Journoud's starting point here is a reaction against surrealism and what he perceives to be its compositional over-reliance on juxtaposition, associative imagery and, crucially, metaphor. It has been against such compositional methods that, since the 1960s, Royet-Journoud has attempted to develop what is often termed a 'literal' practice. In part, Royet-Journoud has attempted to develop such a practice by effacing his writing until the published works come to resemble something like minimalism: the white of the page is everywhere and is part of both the poem's form and content; but Royet-Journoud has also developed a poetic—similar to that of Zukofsky but also to the very late Beckett works such as *Worstward Ho* or 'What is the Word'—which relies heavily on the repeated use of the preposition as poetic anchor and foil to language's propensity to combine and sprawl. A preposition, in other words, is not sense itself but a companion to sense. Here 'companion' should be understood only in its nautical sense, namely, as a window frame through which light passes to a lower cabin, and back again. It is the place of foreignness and the foreignness of place. Royet-Journoud's work stands out most in its attempt to establish a literary form which shows chaos, all the attendant mess, the come and go of things, more as they are than as they appear. In interview Royet-Journoud puts it in the following terms: 'my work points to the imperceptible […] I play on minimal units of meaning […] The other constraint, perhaps more delicate in nature, is the avoidance of assonance, alliteration, metaphor: everything that usually represents struggle within a poem […] For me what is interesting is the literal and not the metaphoric.'[2] As Royet-Journoud goes on to develop elsewhere, 'For me, Eluard's verse "The earth is blue like an orange" can be exhausted, it annihilates itself in an excess of meaning. Whereas Marcelin Pleynet's "the far wall is a whitewashed wall" is and remains,

---

[1] Claude Royet-Journoud, *Le Renversement* (Paris: Gallimard, 1972) p.43.
[2] Serge Gavronsky, *Towards a New Poetics: Contemporary Writing in France* (Berkeley, CA: University of California Press, 1994), pp.117-118.

by its very exactness, and evidently within its context, paradoxically indeterminate as to meaning and so will always "vehiculate" narrative.'[3]

In her essay on the poetics of Claude Royet-Journoud and Anne-Marie Albiach, 'Shall We Escape Analogy', Waldrop writes that 'for the long stretch from Romanticism through Modernism, poetry has been more or less identified with metaphor, with relation by analogy. In linguistic terms, this has been an emphasis on the vertical axis of the speech act: the axis of selection, of reference to the code with its vertical substitution-sets of elements linked by similarity, rather than on the horizontal axis of combination, context, contiguity, syntax, and metonymy.'[4] As Fred Orton comments, metonymy 'is based on a proposed continuous or sequential link between the literal object and its replacement by association or reference.' Crucially, metonymy is 'the record of a lacuna, of a move or displacement from cause to effect, container to contained.' In other words, metonymy 'represents not the object or thing or event or feeling which is its referent but that which is tied to it by contingent or associative transfers of meaning.'[5]

For Waldrop, to attempt to write on the basis of this metonymic horizontal axis is to hold 'a view of the poem as constructing a world through its process, rather than expressing or representing an experience or world existing prior to its formulation.'[6] On Waldrop's reading, the aesthetic interest of this horizontal axis is that it leads away from traditional notions of poetic device to a sense of the poem as, first and foremost, architectural. As Waldrop puts it with reference to Royet-Journoud, 'the spatial arrangement is used to establish relations between terms and to replace, as much as possible, relation by metaphor or other forms of analogy.'[7] This 'as much as possible' is key: Waldrop knows it is not possible to escape metaphorical discourse entirely, that 'every linguistic act involves *both* selection from the code, the vertical substitution-sets, *and* combination in the horizontal dimension of

---

[3] Mathieu Bénézet, 'Claude Royet-Journoud Interviewed,' *Shearsman*, No.2 (1981) p.58 [pp.56-58].
[4] Waldrop, 'Shall We Escape Analogy,' p.105.
[5] Fred Orton, 'Present, the Sense of ... Selves, the Occasion of ... Ruses,' in *Foirades/Fizzles: Echo and Allusion in the Art of Jasper Johns*, ed. James Cuno (Los Angeles: The Grunewald Center for the Graphic Arts and Wight Art Gallery at UCLA, 1987) p.172; quoted in Marjorie Perloff, *Frank O'Hara: Poet Among Painters* (Chicago and London: The University of Chicago Press, 1998) p.xxii.
[6] Waldrop, 'Shall We Escape Analogy,' p.105.
[7] ibid, p.107.

contiguity.'[8] But knowing this does not preclude the attempt to do something different, something else, with language; as Waldrop notes, it is about putting the '*emphasis* more on one axis than on the other.'[9] Here the most pressing question becomes methodological, namely, how should one write such that primary emphasis is placed on the horizontal axis of contiguity rather than the vertical axis of relation? How sidestep the common drive of language towards equivalence?

Waldrop first outlines her notion of contiguity in 1971 in her monograph *Against Language?*. It is, Waldrop argues, a poetic model of composition that emerges in opposition to the increasingly dominant prevalence of the expressive lyric and metaphor as the basis of poetry from Romantic poetry onwards. In opposition to the post-Romantic 'stress on expressiveness and the conception of the poet as *vates*,' Waldrop argues, the 'preference of contiguity implies stress on composition and the conception of the poet as *faber*, as craftsman.'[10]

Waldrop goes on largely to outline metonymic works of German poetry, alongside various theories of language, with a particular emphasis on how twentieth-century poets experiment with language use. As Waldrop puts it in the introduction, she is not concerned with the pragmatic aspect of the linguistic sign, with breakdown of communication, but with poetic technique that affects language. 'And I mean language in the most basic sense: the words, the reference code, and the rules for combination that a given language uses.'[11] As Waldrop goes on to specify, much of her central interest concerns the ways in which such linguistically innovative poetry 'seems to demand a symbolic interpretation and yet refuses it. It attracts our attention to that which it does NOT do. It does not allow us to overlook the refusal of going beyond the structure, of metaphoric transference, of similarity.'[12]

In her 1977 essay, 'Charles Olson: Process and Relationship,' Waldrop further elaborates these ideas, quoting Olson's principle that '[a]t root (or stump) what *is*, is no longer THINGS but what happens BETWEEN things.'[13] Similarly, as Ernest Fenollosa wrote in *Notes on the Chinese Written Character*, and which, Waldrop notes, Olson

---

[8] ibid, p.117.
[9] ibid, p.117.
[10] Waldrop, *Against Language?*, p.123.
[11] ibid, p.12.
[12] ibid, p.88.
[13] Waldrop, 'Charles Olson: Process and Relationship,' p.60.

underlined in his copy: 'A true noun, an isolated thing, does not exist in nature. Things are only terminal points, or rather the meeting points, of actions, cross-sections cut through actions, snap-shots [...] thing and action cannot be separated.'[14] And as Waldrop goes on to gloss in what can equally be read as an early statement of her own developing poetic principle: 'what matters is what happens *between* things, *between* words. You cannot separate things and actions, you cannot separate an occasion into its discrete components.'[15]

And yet nor can those components be conflated or rendered the same. Olson may well famously maintain that 'ONE PERCEPTION MUST IMMEDIATELY AND DIRECTLY LEAD TO A FURTHER PERCEPTION' but from there it does not necessarily follow that that sequential movement is orchestrated by a pattern of cause and effect.[16] For Olson, as for Waldrop, rather, any sequence is contiguous, discrete, non-associative. It is so, Waldrop suggests, because here 'the direction is outward and physical, towards perceptions rather than ideas,' but also because it establishes a pattern of movement which has 'no "organic" closure,' that can 'go on forever' and that 'is definitely "open"':

> Even the balance of forces that tells writer and reader that the poem is finished is temporary. On contact with, in the neighbourhood of, another poem the balance proves to have vectors toward yet further perceptions.[17]

In many ways, this suspicion of equivalence can be understood as a suspicion of knowledge, or more properly, a suspicion of claims to knowledge. As Olson put it in a letter to Cid Corman, 'one can only express that which he knows. Now the further difficulty is, we think we know. And that too is a mare's nest: we don't even know until we bend to the modesty to say we have nothing to say.'[18]

Indeed, in Olson's language, equivalence is a closed field. Rather than necessarily illuminating the world, however, contiguity caters for doubt: as a relation *between* terms it makes no totalising claim. In

---

[14] Ernest Fenollosa, *The Chinese Written Character as a Medium for Poetry* (San Francisco: City Lights, 1964) p.10; also quoted in Waldrop, 'Charles Olson: Process and Relationship,' p.61.
[15] Waldrop, 'Charles Olson: Process and Relationship,' p.61
[16] Charles Olson, 'Projective Verse,' p.17.
[17] Waldrop, 'Charles Olson: Process and Relationship,' pp.61-62.
[18] Charles Olson, 'Letter to Cid Corman,' 26 January 1953, in *Letters for Origin: 1950-1955*, ed. Albert Glover (London: Cape Goliard, 1969) p.120.

Being Singular Plural Jean-Luc Nancy develops this sense of contiguity, arguing that contiguity establishes a discrete chain of singularities which are non-continuous with one another. 'From one singular to another,' Nancy writes, 'there is contiguity but not continuity. There is proximity, but only to the extent that extreme closeness emphasizes the distancing it opens up.'[19] Nancy goes on to develop this argument by suggesting the ways in which the proximity yet non-equivalence of singular contiguities corresponds to the space of the between. As Nancy puts it, the between has 'neither a consistency nor continuity of its own. It does not lead from one to the other; it constitutes no connective tissue, no cement, no bridge.'[20] Rather, analogous to the 'strands whose extremities remain separate even at the very center of the knot [...] the "between" is the stretching out and distance opened by the singular as such, as its spacing of meaning.'[21]

For Waldrop it is the clash of singular, and singularly imperfect, edges that figures the world, in the kind of jarring that exposes loose ends. 'In terms of language,' Waldrop writes, 'it means attention to sentence and sequence.'[22] It is, in other words, first and foremost a formal question, a question of finding a form that projects outward, that layers and lays down a topography manifold and open on all sides. It means establishing a poetic method aimed at the adjacent rather than the equivalent. It means finding a way to show, in language, in form, how one perception follows another perception but that they are not the same and that there is no necessary correspondence, causal or otherwise, between the two. It means 'not growing inward, deeper, by finding more to say about the same thing, metaphors for it, symbols, analogies,' Waldrop writes in the wake of Olson's poetics, 'but instead turning to the adjoining thing, contiguity, further perceptions;'[23] it means 'exploring the sentence and its boundaries, slidings, the gaps between fragments, the shadow zone of silence, of margins.'[24] It means all this because, as Waldrop quotes from William Carlos Williams' *Paterson*, in a phrase which also lends Waldrop the title for her collected essays:

---

[19] Jean-Luc Nancy, *Being Singular Plural*, trans. Robert D. Richardson and Anne E. O'Byrne (Stanford, CA: Stanford University Press, 2000), p.5.
[20] ibid, p.4.
[21] ibid, p.5.
[22] Waldrop, 'Charles Olson: Process and Relationship,' p.66.
[23] ibid, pp.69-70.
[24] Waldrop, 'Form and Discontent,' p.200.

Dissonance
(if you are interested)
leads to discovery[25]

Elsewhere Waldrop argues that there are four main implications to this emphasis on the contiguous:

1. Nothing is given. (Though all the elements are: there is nothing new under the sun.) Everything remains to be constructed.
2. The poet does not know beforehand what the poem is going to say, where the poem is going to take her [...] The poem is not so much 'expression' as a cognitive process that, to some extent, changes even the poet.
3. The aim is not unifying (the one right word, the one perfect metaphor), but to open the form to the multiplicity of contexts.
4. The transcendence is not upward, but horizontal, contextual. It is the transcendence of language with its infinite possibilities, infinite connections, and its charge of the past. In other words, no split between subject and matter.[26]

Such a horizontal writing corresponds to what might be termed a non-representational communication, a formal filtering of something that withholds itself, that hides within the folds of its own address. Such a filtering corresponds to a form at least, if not a language, of surfaces. At issue here is what might be termed the stubborn singularity of a literal writing, in the sense that literality is to be understood as that which refuses to exhibit anything other than itself. In this way, a literal writing is nothing more than a writing of letters that stall in advance the cumulative processes of discourse and intelligibility. What remains is simply the blank expression of what appears on the page. As Emmanuel Hocquard has illustratively commented, 'When I say that what I write is literal [...] I simply mean that my articulations are intended to be taken to the letter, as they are reproduced in black and white.'[27]

The consequence of such an understanding of literal writing is that there is nothing to be done with it. Literality as compositional method

---

[25] Williams, *Paterson*, p.176; quoted in Waldrop, *Lavish Absence* p.45.
[26] Waldrop, 'Form and Discontent,' p.203.
[27] Emmanuel Hocquard, 'This Story that is Mine' in *Crosscut Universe: Writing on Writing From France*, ed. Norma Cole (Providence: Burning Deck, 2000) p.98.

is concerned not with communication but with the vacant space these letters partially cover over. In this way, the poem does not produce a document but simply inscribes, in a neutral register, the absence of documentation. Following on from this, if the poem can be said to produce anything at all, it would be only the deferral of production. As Joseph Guglielmi puts it, it is '[a]s if suspicion of the letter in its regulated sense wanted, through innovative tension, to precipitate the course of the shattering and the flagrant diversion of the forbidden.'[28] 'This glint of light on the cut is what I'm after,' writes Waldrop. 'Juxtaposing, rather than isolating, minimal units of meaning.'[29] And here the 'transcendence is not upward, but horizontal, contextual. It is the transcendence of language with its infinite possibilities, infinite connections, and its charge of the past.'[30]

Shifting the emphasis from similarity to contiguity highlights both the importance and the implications of between. It is about exploring the working of language and of things, of seeing what happens, what comes out. 'And the shards catch light on the cut, [and] the edges give off sparks.'[31] As Waldrop puts it in relation to her novel, *The Hanky of Pippin's Daughter*, 'as soon as you put down one element you start limiting the options. A "then" implies a temporal sequence, maybe even a causal one, which is what the novel supposedly works with. But the holes are actually more important. The holes, all that escapes the story, the unrealized potential of the narrative.'[32] 'Everything remains to be constructed.'[33]

Beckett on Joyce: 'Here form *is* content, content *is* form. You complain that this stuff is not written in English. It is not written at all. It is not to be read—or rather it is not only to be read. It is to be looked at and listened to. His writing is not *about* something, *it is that something itself.*'[34]

---

[28] Joseph Guglielmi, 'The Radical Cut' in *Crosscut Universe*, p. 79.
[29] Waldrop, 'Thinking of Follows,' p.210.
[30] Waldrop, 'Form and Discontent,' p.203.
[31] Waldrop, *Ceci*, p. 86.
[32] Joan Retallack, 'A Conversation Between Joan Retallack and Rosmarie Waldrop, Pt.2,' *How2*, Vol. 1, No. 8 (Fall, 2002), http://www.asu.edu/pipercwcenter/how2journal/archive/online_archive/v1_8_2002/current/readings/retallack.htm, accessed 7 August 2012.
[33] Waldrop, 'Form and Discontent,' p.203.
[34] Samuel Beckett, 'Dante… Bruno. Vico… Joyce,' *Disjecta: Miscellaneous Writings and a Dramatic Fragment*, ed. Ruby Cohn (London: John Calder, 1983) p.14.

Hugo von Hofmannsthal: 'We must hide what is deep. Where? On the surface.'[35]

---

[35] Quoted in Waldrop, *Ceci*, p.91.

The Caesura

In many ways, it is largely for this reason that Waldrop has referred to the caesura as another example of the empty centre in her work.[1]

In the move from the clipped line of her early poetry to her later prose poetry and engagements with the structure of the sentence, Waldrop relocates the tension from the edge of the line to the inside of the sentence: 'the tensions could happen inside it, between one sentence and the next, between it and grammatical norms.'[2] Most frequently, but perhaps with a marked escalation of compositional and conceptual importance since the publication of *Blindsight* in 2003, Waldrop's central method for rendering this internal tension has been through the recurrent and grammatically disruptive use of the period or full-stop. As Marjorie Perloff has commented of the frequently arrested movement of Waldrop's sentences, with specific reference to the 1994 sequence 'Split Infinites,' 'the forward momentum of the sentence is constantly halted by repetition, variation, sound, echo, and interruption. Again and again, this form implies, one tries to arrest the "split infinites" of one's existence in such faux closural units of thought only to discover that the neat unit cannot contain the experience.'[3]

Similarly, in relation to the musical compositions of Gordon Mumma, Robert Ashley, and John Cage, as well as the choreography of Merce Cunningham, Waldrop describes such a method as an 'aleatory grammar, a decentering, an out-of-phase syntax.'[4] In her 1934 lecture, 'Poetry and Grammar,' Gertrude Stein puts better than most the essentials at stake:

> What had periods to do with it. Inevitably no matter how completely I had to have writing go on, physically one had to again and again stop sometime and if one had to again and again stop sometime then periods had to exist. Besides I had always liked the look of periods and I liked what they did. Stopping sometime did not really keep one from going

---

[1] Waldrop, 'The Ground is the Only Figure,' p.250.
[2] ibid, p.267.
[3] Marjorie Perloff, 'A Small Periplus Along an Edge: Rosmarie Waldrop's AutoGraphs,' *How2*, Vol.1, No.8 (Fall, 2002), http://www.asu.edu/pipercwcenter/how2journal/archive/online_archive/v1_8_2002/current/readings/perloff.htm, accessed 5 July 2012.
[4] Waldrop, 'Between, Always,' 271.

on, it was nothing that interfered, it was only something that happened, and as it happened as a perfectly natural happening, I did believe in periods and I used them.[5]

The period, in other words, enables an anti-linear sequence of sentences, phrases, clauses; it enables continuity even as connectives are displaced, development in the form of fragmentation; it registers the different in the same. 'Tension is also one of the ways we can talk about rhythm. As long as you write in a regular meter you can talk about rhythm in terms of the tension between the meter and "normal" speech. In free verse, in terms of the tension between line and sentence. But in prose poems? I've recently used periods as rhythmic markers rather than, or in addition to, using them as grammatical markers: "How the words are. Suspended around you."'[6] Here the full stop acts as a measure of breath, a rhythm, both a spacing and a pacing, what Edmond Jabès terms a text's folding in on itself, where 'breath becomes shorter, breathing becomes difficult.'[7]

The example of Gertrude Stein, along with that of the avant-garde German poet, Helmut Heissenbüttel, was a formative early influence on Waldrop's engagement with the caesura as both formal and conceptual strategy. In general Stein's and Heissenbüttel's influence primarily related to the problematic of naming that features so prominently in their respective poetics, but more particularly it had to do with both the effects and the implications of their various strategies for problematising the basic grammatical pattern of subject-predicate-object. 'The difference,' Stein once famously remarked, 'is spreading.'[8] Or as Stein phrased it in her typically idiosyncratic lecture from 1926, 'Composition as Explanation':

> The only thing that is different from one time to another is what is seen and what is seen depends upon how everybody is doing everything. This makes the thing we are looking at very different and this makes what those who describe it make

---

[5] Gertrude Stein, 'Poetry and Grammar,' *Writings and Lectures: 1909-1945*, ed. Patricia Meyerowitz (New York: Penguin, 1971) p.130.
[6] Hulme, 'Interview with Rosmarie Waldrop,' p.79.
[7] Paul Auster, 'Interview with Edmond Jabès,' *The Sin of the Book*, ed. Eric Gould (Lincoln: University of Nebraska Press), p.15; quoted in Waldrop, *Lavish Absence*, p.9.
[8] Stein, *Tender Buttons*, p.7.

of it, it makes a composition, it confuses, it shows, it is, it looks, it likes it as it is, and this makes what is seen as it is seen. Nothing changes from generation to generation except the thing seen and that makes a composition.[9]

The insistence of Stein's indirect nouns here are at once obfuscating and telling. As Bruce Bassoff has commented, throughout both this essay and her writing more generally Stein's emphasis is not 'on individual elements, which remain the same, but on the relations between those elements, which change.'[10] Stein's infamous statement that 'a rose is a rose is a rose' which she later had inscribed in an endless loop on a signet ring, is an even clearer instance of what is at stake. As numerous commentators have outlined, what matters most is the utterance of the third 'rose' such that its third repetition 'defies both a tradition of conventional grammar and an illusion that language is simply a transparent medium for communicating perceptions and ideas.'[11] That supplementary rose, in other words, illuminates language itself, language as material, as density. Stein herself put it in the following terms: 'When I said, "A rose is a rose is a rose," and later made that into a ring, I made poetry and what did I do I caressed completely caressed and addressed a noun.'[12] In other words, Stein addressed a world of words, or better, the world as word, with only sediments of grammar. As Bruce Andrews has noted, 'Signs usually stabilized by customary use get shaken up by a materiality that miniaturizes its possible uses. The normative confinements of grammar and narrative and self-expression give way to even more forceful and disabling vectors. We get a language almost beyond linguistics. We're not looking through the words, with the trappings of perspective, once the language is no longer pointing, offering a stand-in, or a representative.'[13]

In Heissenbüttel this empty centre takes the form of a linguistic opacity, a process of writing which layers clause upon clause without

---

[9] Stein, 'Compositon as Explanation,' p.497.
[10] Bruce Bassoff, 'Gertrude Stein's "Composition as Explanation,"' *Twentieth Century Literature*, Vol. 24, No.1 (Spring, 1978) p.76 [pp.76-80].
[11] Steven Gould Axelrod et al., *Modernisms: 1900-1950*, Vol.2 (New Brunswick, NJ: Rutgers University Press, 2007) p.90.
[12] Gertrude Stein, 'Poetry and Grammar' in *Lectures in America* (New York: Random House, 1935) p.231.
[13] Bruce Andrews, 'Reading Language, Reading Gertrude Stein,' *Pores* 3 (2001), reprinted at: http://www.pores.bbk.ac.uk/3/andrews.html, accessed 17 May 2011.

any clear resolution or identification. Sentences sprawl but are never fixed. As Waldrop puts it in *Against Language?* Heissenbüttel's poetry 'seems to move right on the borderline of "significance". It seems to demand a symbolic interpretation and yet refuses it.'[14] It does so because, in Heissenbüttel, the all important noun remains either vague or absent and his poetry becomes one of structure rather than metaphor. Composition is explanation and the poetry works by indirection. As Heissenbüttel puts it, 'Sentence subjects, sentence objects, sentence predicates are omitted because experience talked about stands outside the clear-cut subject-object relation. Only a formulation that leaves open one of the elements of the old basic model can say anything about it.'[15] Heissenbüttel's poem *Endlösung*, 'Final Solution', is perhaps one of the most startling and striking examples of the affect of this kind of writing. To take one sample paragraph, from the middle of the poem:

> they thought it up and they hit on it when they wanted to start something but what they hit on wasn't something you could be for but you could be against or better yet something you could get most people to be against because when you can get most people to be against something you don't have to be very specific about what you can be for and the fact that you don't have to be very specific about this has its advantages because as long as they can let off steam most people don't care what they are for[16]

As Waldrop notes, 'here Hitler's "final solution" for the Jews is talked about without being mentioned, except in the title [...] The power lies exactly in the fact that the text does not state what it was "they" thought up, what it was they could get people to be against. Nothing but this circling around an unnamed middle could convey so much ambivalence.'[17]

What particularly appeals to Waldrop about this model of writing is the way in which Heissenbüttel works with grammatically correct sentences but which 'have only very vague meaning because they have

---

[14] Waldrop, *Against Language?*, p.88.
[15] Helmut Heisenbüttel, *Über Literatur*, p.223; quoted in Waldrop, 'Helmut Heissenbüttel, Poet of Contexts,' *Dissonance*, p.17.
[16] Quoted in Waldrop, *Dissonance*, p.27. For a longer translation of this poem, see Waldrop's 'Alarms and Excursions,' *Dissonance*, pp.176-77.
[17] Waldrop, 'Helmut Heissenbüttel, Poet of Contexts,' p.27.

no nouns, no specific names.'[18] As Waldrop puts it with regards to her own work, her growing interest in the semantic and conceptual possibilities of subordinate clauses, digressions, 'meanders, space to amble', highlighted the sentence as the principle staging ground for these concerns: the tension she had previously highlighted in her work through the use of short lines, through the simultaneous pull between flow and fragment, the ongoing rush between object and subject, was shifted to the inside of the sentence, 'between one sentence and the next, between it and grammatical norms.'[19]

Caesura as break, as clinamen: 'For a fraction of a moment, this void stops everything. It suspends the assurance of statement to reintroduce uncertainty, possibility, and potential. According to Friedrich Hölderlin, the gap of the caesura, metrical poetry's additional locus of disjunction, blocks the hypnotic enchantment of rhythm and images: "the caesura (the counter-rhythmic interruption) becomes necessary to block the torrential succession of representations [...] in such a way as to make manifest [...] representation itself.'[20] For Waldrop, in other words, the caesura is a 'void that shows representation [...] language itself.' 'In addition,' Waldrop continues, 'a bit more tangibly, it lets us feel the magnetic field between the two dimensions, energy's horizontal push becomes dammed up, vertical, orchestral, an aura.'[21]

'I break up sentences with periods. Partly as rhythmic measure. Like the end of a line does in verse. But it also sometimes allows a double-construction of what it could mean.'[22]

For Joan Retallack, 'Waldrop composes the cultural flotsam and jetsam out of which we fabricate memory into shifting mosaics whose energy derives from interactions of textual particles (captions, lists, anecdotal fragments, descriptive glimpses—data of various, humorous sorts) and narrative/speculative waves that raise questions about our relation to art, science, politics, history.'[23]

'The displacement matters less to me,' Waldrop comments, 'than the glint of light on the cut, the edges radiating energy. The fragmentary, "torn" nature of the elements.'[24] Or as Emmanuel Hocquard has it,

---

[18] ibid, p.17.
[19] Waldrop, 'Between, Always,' p.267.
[20] Waldrop, 'Why Do I Write Prose Poems,' p.261.
[21] ibid, p.261.
[22] Demick, 'Interview with Keith and Rosmarie Waldrop Interview.'
[23] Joan Retallack, 'A Conversation,' p.330.
[24] Waldrop, 'Why Do I Write Prose Poems,' p.263.

the caesura, like fragments, should be considered openings onto new connections, new possibilities, networks and sites of crossing, relation, rather than as something incomplete, broken, partially lost.[25]

In the words of Philippe Lacoue-Labarthe, the caesura is to be understood as that which functions as a kind of 'general logic of differentiation', a 'regulated contradiction' which produces 'the exchange or the passage into the opposite.'[26] The basis of Lacoue-Labarthe's reading of the caesura here comes from Hölderlin's notion that the caesura is 'an antirhythmic interruption' which enables an 'onrushing alternation of representations [...] in such a way that it is no longer the alternation of representations, but rather the representation itself which appears.'[27] Lacoue-Labarthe goes on to develop this sense of the caesura by explaining that 'such a disarticulation of the work and of the process of succession through alternations which constitutes the work as such [...] does not suppress the logic of exchange and alternation. It simply brings it to a halt.' 'It prevents it,' Lacoue-Labarthe continues, 'from exhibiting its representations in one sense or another.' And as Lacoue-Labarthe summarises in words which are also directly applicable to Waldrop's poetic process and her concentration on the between as both ground and figure, 'it avoids [...] the inflection toward this or that pole. The disarticulation represents the active neutrality of that which is in between both poles.' It is, in other words, 'an empty moment.'[28]

Waldrop's 2003 sequence, 'Hölderlin Hybrids,' is a case in point, particularly in terms of its repeated use of the caesura as a device to weave two disparate texts by Hölderlin and Yoel Hoffmann together. As Deborah Meadows sets out, the sequence develops Waldrop's earlier 'examination of cultural and social encoding at the level of the sentence toward a use of the sentence-level tension that breaks into gaps punctuated by full stop periods.'[29] The first section of 'Hölderlin Hybrids' begins thus:

---

[25] See Emmanuel Hocquard, *Le Voyage à Reykjavik* (Paris: P.O.L., 1997) p.12.
[26] Philippe Lacoue-Labarthe, 'The Caesura of the Speculative,' in Samuel Weber and Henry Sussman (eds.), *Glyph 4* (Baltimore and London: The Johns Hopkins University Press, 1978) p.60.
[27] Heinrich Hölderlin, quoted in Lacoue-Labarthe, 'The Caesura,' p.83.
[28] Lacoue-Labarthe, 'The Caesura,' p.83.
[29] Deborah Meadows, 'Reading Rosmarie Waldrop and Yoel Hoffmann,' *Another Language: Poetic Experiments in Britain and North America*, ed. Kornelia Freitag and Katharina Vester (Münster: Lit Verlag, 2008), p.152.

> The world was galaxies imagined flesh. Mortal. What to think now? Think simple. Matter? A lump of wax? An afterglow? Or does everything happen of its own accord? Perfect and full-bodied. No more. Observable. No longer. In your eyes or line of sight. Down all three dimensions of time. Or lock up the house. Or prophets.[30]

All flows, of language, thought, experience, are interrupted, even while at the same time each interruption actually serves to propel the poem forward. It is a poetry of simultaneous breaks and assemblages, a way of building by degrees; a way of building which is always open, ajar, attentive to an essential ambiguity. As Rosmarie and Keith put in their preface to the Burning Deck anthology, *A Century in Two Decades*, 'it is not denying the importance of "movements," to insist that there is another importance in moving beside or apart from them.'[31]

---

[30] Waldrop, *Blindsight*, p.3.
[31] Rosmarie and Keith Waldrop, *A Century in Two Decades*, p.9.

Poetry and Politics

Following the terrorist attacks on the World Trade Center on September 11, 2001, Anna Rabinowitz, the editor of *American Letters & Commentary*, invited responses to the following:

> After WWII Theodor Adorno famously declared that to write poetry after Auschwitz is barbaric, to which Edmond Jabès less famously replied: "I say that after Auschwitz we must write poetry but with wounded words." We want to ask the following questions:
> 1. What do we as writers do at times when our modes of speech and even language itself seem incapable of making meaning?
> 2. How can we adapt our defeated, exhausted language to something fresh and clear-sighted, to something that can carry the human narration/commentary forward when conditions themselves are unspeakable?
> 3. What wellsprings can we draw upon to refresh the always living, always dying word?
> 4. Do we need to explore or develop new ways of reading as well as writing?[1]

Waldrop's response to this invitation was to write a short essay entitled 'Nothing to Say and Saying It.' In that essay Waldrop sketches the basis of an emergent poetics that exemplifies a notion of human relationality premised on what she terms 'encounter rather than domination or confrontation.'[2] Waldrop goes on to quote a passage from Giorgio Agamben's *Means without Ends*:

> We can communicate with others only through what in us—as much as in others—has remained potential, and any communication is first of all communication not of something but of communicability itself. After all, if there existed one and only one being, it would be absolutely impotent [...] And where I am capable, we are always already many.[3]

---

[1] Anna Rabinowitz, *American Letters & Commentary*, quoted in Waldrop, 'Nothing to Say and Saying It,' *Dissonance*, p.274.
[2] Waldrop, 'Nothing to Say,' p. 277.
[3] Giorgio Agamben, *Means Without End*, trans. Vincenzo Binetti and Cesare Casarino (Minneapolis: University of Minnesota Press, 2000) p.9.

Waldrop reads this passage as 'an imperative to guard against our thinking becoming fixed in ideologies and -isms (including patriotism), to cultivate our potential, our openness.'[4] Waldrop insists, in other words, that Agamben's notion of relation points to a prohibition against any form of private estate. In this context Waldrop goes on to argue that the task of the poet is to work toward the emergence of a language that unravels itself. Yet she also states that her own poetic response to 9/11 did not succeed. 'Words,' she writes, 'fail us in shock, in horror, in the face of death.'[5] Indeed, it is in view of this apparent 'failure of words' that Waldrop opens her essay with John Cage's statement that 'Poetry is having nothing to say, and saying it.' As Waldrop comments, 'I identify with Cage's position. The first part of his statement is my constant experience. I've felt it when I tried to write a poem "about" 9/11.'[6]

The poem Waldrop is referring to here is 'Disaster,' published as the final sequence in the 2003 collection, *Love, Like Pronouns*. What particularly stands out about this poem is the way in which Waldrop, having nothing to say, attempts to say nothing about 9/11, and how saying nothing critically frames and bears upon her own consideration of the space of the political in the poem. While Waldrop's poem 'Disaster' is discursively structured around representations of and responses to the attack on the Word Trade Centre in New York on 11 September 2001, particularly striking is the way in which the specific hinge of 'Disaster' is in fact the interval of the page, the blind spot where all representations and responses cease. This is not to say that the tragedy of those attacks becomes merely a vehicle for reflection or that the poem's content is either subordinate to or differential from the specific property of the page. Much of Waldrop's frame of reference is underpinned by her reading of the American poet Andrew Joron's short essay 'The Emergency,' which deals with the social-political climate of a post-9/11 America and, specifically, the relationship between poetry and politics.

First published as a pamphlet entitled 'The Emergency of Poetry' in 2002, republished as the opening section to his 2003 collection *Fathom*, and then again in the 2007 prose collection, *The Cry at Zero*, Joron's essay threads a deliberately uneven, yet also sometimes uneasy,

---

[4] Waldrop, 'Nothing to Say,' p. 277.
[5] ibid, p.276.
[6] ibid, p.275.

line between ellipsis, speculation and polemic.[7] At the time of writing, Joron comments, 'public space in the United States is bedecked with flags, colorfully curtaining the contradictions of the "war against terrorism" [...] "America stands united," yet remains a divided and antagonistic society.'[8] Although, Joron quickly continues, that 'the atrocities committed on 9/11' defy justification, the focus of his critique is the nature of America's political and military response to those acts of violence.[9] In Joron's terms, although '[t]hese horrific acts constituted nothing less than crimes against humanity [...] the U.S. was obligated, morally and politically, not to respond in kind.'[10]

Joron is arguing for a mode of response that, before anything, is issued both linguistically and conceptually from responsibility. For Joron, by responding 'in kind' with what he terms 'annihilative vengeance', the American political, military and cultural landscape exhibits what Derrida has referred to as a process of 'auto-immunity'.[11] In other words, through strategies of 'vengeance' and 'pre-emption', for Joron the American state comes to display pathological symptoms, such that its means of self-protection become self-consumptive. In such a situation, Derrida writes:

> What will never let itself be forgotten is thus the perverse effect of the autoimmunitary itself [...] repression in both its psychoanalytical sense and its political sense—whether it be through the police, the military, or the economy—ends up producing, reproducing, and regenerating the very thing it seeks to disarm.[12]

Joron then offers this subsequent diagnosis: 'Violence of this order must take its toll on the life-world of the destroyer-nation itself. A harsh, acrid odor begins to seep through the walls, spoiling works of art,' to

---

[7] Andrew Joron, 'The Emergency' in *Fathom* (Black Square Editions, 2003) pp. 15-25. See also, Joron, *The Cry at Zero: Selected Prose* (Denver, CO: Counterpath Press, 2007), pp.1-10.
[8] ibid, p.16.
[9] ibid, p.17.
[10] ibid, p.17.
[11] ibid, p.17.
[12] Jacques Derrida, in Giovanna Borradori (ed.), *Philosophy in a Time of Terror* (Chicago and London: The University of Chicago Press) p.99. For Derrida's initial discussion of 'auto-immunity', see 'Faith and Knowledge' in *Acts of Religion* (ed. Gil Anidjar), (London and New York: Routledge, 2002) p.80, n. 27.

the extent that, for Joron, '"culture" has been reduced to a simple play of intensities, to the simultaneously brutal and sentimental pulsions of mass media.'[13] And then, Joron adds, 'American poetry is a marginal genre whose existence is irrelevant to the course of Empire.'[14]

While taking its cue from contemporary events, it is worth remarking that Joron's argument here is more familiar than it is radically cutting edge. On one level at least, it largely rehearses in miniature a long-standing aesthetic tradition that considers the degrees of correspondence and separation between aesthetics and the modern world in the Continental tradition. Such a debate is at the centre of the Jena school's reflections on the philosophy of art, of Hölderlin's poetics, of Keats, Nietzsche, of Heidegger's writings on art and poetry, of Theodor Adorno, and so on. Joron himself deliberately registers such a genealogy at the very outset of 'The Emergency' when, in a clear echo of Heidegger's citation of Hölderlin at the opening of 'What are Poets For?', Joron asks 'What good is poetry at a time like this?'[15] For Joron, as for Heidegger and Hölderlin before him, the contemporary period is destitute and it is this destitution that becomes the principle condition of poetry.

At least one of the questions such a framework immediately raises, however, is at once straightforward and complex. In other words, in such a social-political context, why ask this question of poetry? Why speculate on the worth of poetry at a time like this? And, even if it is relevant, what might this poetry look like and read like and sound like, and so on, and even so?

As Joron comments:

> It feels right to ask this question [of the worth of poetry at a time like this], and at the same time to resist the range of predictable answers, such as: Poetry is useless, therein lies its freedom. Or, poetry has the power to expose ideology; gives a voice to that which has been denied a voice; serves as a call to action; consoles and counsels; keeps the spirit alive.[16]

It is noticeable that Joron doesn't actually explain why it apparently feels right to ask this question of poetry. Yet it is precisely this gap

---
[13] Joron, 'The Emergency,' p.17.
[14] ibid, p.18.
[15] ibid, p.15.
[16] ibid, p.15.

between the question and the apparent requirement to ask it that Joron will later come to mime throughout the essay, finding poetry there, in the space between the one and the other. It is also the reason why, for Joron, each of the standard responses to the question of the good of poetry is correct but somehow inadequate, off the point, off kilter. Like Waldrop, in Joron's view, poetry is somewhere else, it is an alternative discourse, a discourse of alternatives, unwriting or writing out, over, any possible interchange between question and response. 'Poetry cannot be anything,' Joron maintains, 'other than inadequate, even to itself.'[17]

From such an unequivocal statement, then, it necessarily follows that, first and foremost, 'what good is poetry at a time like this' has to be understood simply as an inadequate question. It may well raise something about poetry and the contemporary world, but it does so largely by suggesting the two have little in common. Aesthetic questions of poetic practice tend to fall outside the confines of more apparently immediately urgent questions of the state of the contemporary, and as such poetry largely falls flat, out of itself, into muffling, muting, a dulling down the drain. Yet for Joron such a failure actually constitutes the very form and function of poetry today. As he writes:

> [a] kind of topological fold or failure (called a 'catastrophe' in mathematics) precedes the emergence—constitutes the emergency—of the New. If poetry 'makes language new,' then it must be defined as the translation of emergency.[18]

And then, Joron adds, 'even politically engaged poetry cannot escape this consequence. The abyssal language of poetry represents (translates) the motion of social change more than it does the facts of social change.'[19]

Two points are particularly resonant here. First, Joron assigns a social role to poetry: in reaching into the abyss, poetry, he argues, mimes a process of social translation. Second, such a process is, at best, marginal: poetic emergence takes place against the grain, off-stage, behind the scenes. As Joron writes in a poem collected in *Fathom* and that serves as a general representation of his wider poetics of emergency:

---

[17] ibid, p.15.
[18] ibid, p.15.
[19] ibid, p.15.

> Imagine the spoken, O's
> Spokes convergent on no center. No place
> Is polis.[20]

For Joron, then, the poetical polis corresponds to an undoing of the polis itself in the sense that poetic terrain not only disorganises or displaces, but, crucially, is displaced by itself. A poetics of emergency is an elsewhere poetics, one that, like the shards of collage, simultaneously appropriates and scatters.

Joron goes on to explain that this expatriated dispersal legitimises the very force and thus 'good' of poetry. As he writes:

> only here, at this very juncture between language and power, can the refused word come back to itself as the word of refusal, as the sign of that which cannot be assimilated to the system—[21]

Joron, in other words, conceives poetry as what he describes as a 'a word beyond meaning.'[22] As a result, for Joron, the non-appropriability of poetry constitutes an act of opening; as he says: 'if only to make an O, an indwelling of zero, an Otherness.'[23] Poetry, he argues in a manner reminiscent of Adorno's reflections on aesthetic theory and the modern world, 'affirms nothing but the negative truth of its non-identity.'[24] It is a 'voiceless voice,' 'fashioned by no one in particular,' 'spontaneously springing forth as pure enigma [...] a surreality.'[25] Joron maintains that 'the *emergence* of this [poetic] object' constitutes nothing less than 'an *emergency* for any restricted economy of meaning.'[26]

In many senses, this interface between emergence and emergency is the crucial element of Joron's argument. He argues that poetic practice constitutes an emergency for the established order for the simple reason that its aesthetic of emergence invalidates normative classifications between here and there, this and that, us and them, and so on. In other words, for Joron, poetry, as that which listens to 'the speechlessness of words,' as a remove that cannot be removed, becomes a privileged

---

[20] Joron, 'Eclipse Calling,' *Fathom*, p.90.
[21] Joron, 'The Emergency,' p.18.
[22] ibid, p.20.
[23] ibid, p.18.
[24] ibid, p.19.
[25] ibid, pp. 20, 15, and 21.
[26] ibid, p.20.

and exceptional site of social, political, and cultural resistance precisely because its 'aesthetics of overloadedness' renders 'the origins of order [...] vertiginous.'[27] Here, Joron's elaboration of 'the good of poetry' is underpinned by Theodor Adorno's sense that 'the most important way to confront the danger of a recurrence is to work against the brute predominance of all collectives.'[28] To do this, Adorno argues, poetic practice 'must turn against itself, in opposition to its own concept, and thus become uncertain of itself right into its innermost fiber.'[29]

According to Joron, such a discordant uncertainty receives its fullest expression in the form of the lament. The reason for this, he argues, is because 'the very bones of language, in which meaning is always displaced from its object, [have] the structure of a lament.'[30] 'The blues, all blues,' he writes, 'are the matrix of the world's subaltern cultures, an expression of triumph in defeat. The raising of the voiceless voice.'[31] As Joron goes on to argue:

> [t]he lament, no less than anger, refuses to accept the fact of suffering. But while anger must possess the stimulus of a proximate cause—or else it eventually fades away—the lament has a universal cause, and rises undiminished through millennia of cultural mediation.[32]

Joron's point here is that the lament corresponds to an archaic yet 'unprecedented Cry.'[33] The contemporary renewal of such a cry, Joron argues, 'would constitute an "ontological turn" away from the epistemological dilemmas of modern and postmodern poetics' toward a form of poetry that incorporates 'the Novum', that is, '*an unexpected, unprecedented superaddition to reality*,' '[t]hat which is radically *other*' and thus does not reveal itself under interrogation.'[34]

Joron's scope is ambitious but there are two particularly resonant ways of developing Joron's notion of the lament in order to outline

---

[27] ibid, pp.16 and 22.
[28] Theodor Adorno, *Critical Models*, trans. Henry W. Pickford (New York: Columbia University Press, 1998) p. 197.
[29] Theodor Adorno, *Aesthetic Theory*, trans. Robert Hullot-Kentor (Minneapolis: University of Minnesota Press, 1997) p. 2.
[30] Joron, 'The Emergency,' p.20.
[31] ibid, p.20.
[32] ibid, p.24.
[33] ibid, p.25.
[34] ibid, pp. 22 and 25.

the terms of Waldrop's own poetics on this subject. The first concerns a certain notion of redemption that intersects illustratively with philosophical, and particularly Adornian, discussions of the messianic; the second in terms of a constitutive interchange between secrecy and communication.

In many respects, Joron's essay wants to suggest that the lament, as Novum or pure emergence, opening, corresponds to a poetics of redemption in the sense that, he writes, this 'poetic opening in the "real world" is a wonderful (meaning miraculous) wound […] it is an act of creation, a sign that the world is not equal to itself.'[35] Adorno's sense of the redemptive prospect of philosophy contains an apposite point of comparison for fully understanding Joron's, and Waldrop's, thinking here. As Adorno writes, 'the only philosophy which can be responsibly practised in face of despair is the attempt to contemplate all things as they would present themselves from the standpoint of redemption.' In order for such a redemptive presentation to occur, he continues:

> perspectives must be fashioned that displace and estrange the world, reveal it to be, with its rifts and crevices, as indigent and distorted as it will appear one day in the messianic light […] It is the simplest of all things, because the situation calls imperatively for such knowledge […] But it is also the utterly impossible thing, because it presupposes a standpoint removed, even by a hair's breadth, from the scope of existence.[36]

In addition to this, however, throughout Joron's text there are also constant echoes and implicit references to the poetic example of Orpheus, as both theme and trope: this Orpheus who looks and, in looking, loses. Just something he does, to measure the mould of motion, a way of focussing, of registering a shape, an other's body, the line of cheek-bone, jut of jaw. And so something he loses because he looks, so that he is compelled to lament, but not in order to memorialise, only for the uncanny reverberation of the cry itself, its gaping O, its secret, such that everything comes down to the name not there, the way it falls out.

As Emmanuel Hocquard writes, 'Orpheus turns. Eurydice is lost to him. And his lament rises into the void opened by what got away.'[37] As

---

[35] ibid, p.19.

[36] Theodor Adorno, *Minima Moralia: Reflections from Damaged Life*, trans. E.F.N. Jephcott (London: Verso, 1978) p.247.

[37] Emmanuel Hocquard, 'This Story that is Mine' in *Crosscut Universe*, p. 97.

Hocquard continues, the object of the lament may well be my secret but it is one where 'my secret does not mean: something I know, that I hide or that I reveal. *My* secret means something escapes *me*'.[38] Read in this context, the lament becomes a non-representational communication, a formal filtering of something that breaks out. It is a form at least, if not a language, of surfaces.

Joron closes 'The Emergency' with a similar principle of innovative tension. The seed of all resistance, he writes, its ratio is: 'O, the grieving vowel' divided by 'zero, the mouth of astonishment [...] In a word, the uncanny reflection of an unfinished world.'[39] The rising shift from word to world that Joron employs here, and repeats again and again in various modes throughout *Fathom*, marks out the question of how to get from 'word' to 'world', highlighting less the incompletion of the world than of the word itself, the rift of its missing letter. In doing so, Joron precipitates the course of the world within the folds of the word's secret letter, of what escapes, of what emerges, of what poetry translates. Its 'myriad displacements' are 'not to be explained' but encountered as fathom, literally, as 'something which embraces' what falls through the cracks, on the edge of writing.[40] As in Emmanuel Levinas' phrase: 'A voice comes from the other shore. A voice interrupts the saying of the already said.'[41]

---

[38] Hocqaurd, 'This Story,' p. 100.
[39] Joron, 'The Emergency,' p.25.
[40] Joron, 'To Be Explained,' *Fathom*, p.82.
[41] Levinas, *Otherwise than Being*, p.183.

Disaster

Waldrop's poem 'Disaster' is everywhere engaged with this question of how to respond to the events of September 11 whereby that sense of response is consistently linked to a critical intersection between an ontology of 'nothing' and a prohibition against representation. Throughout the poem, in other words, the constant threading and unthreading of narrative comes across as an attempt to situate the essential nature of the political as something that resists clear determination. As Waldrop writes at the end of the poem's fourth and final section, '[t]he page is otherwise dark.'[1]

In general terms, 'Disaster' is characterised by the recurring inability to represent, either conceptually or discursively, the fact of the towers' collapse. In part this is because, in the poem, the attack on the World Trade Centre is an event of 'disbelief.' As Waldrop writes in the second section: '[w]e can think away towers. We can think away mountains. Once they're gone we can't. Believe it. We're made to dream dreams of fear.'[2] The ruptured syntax Waldrop employs both here and throughout the sequence is emblematic of the incredulity the poem everywhere articulates. The break between, for instance, 'can't' and 'believe it' both rehearses and exacerbates the stunned and traumatic experience of shock, as well as the historical-political narrative that at once precedes and exceeds the attacks on the World Trade Centre and of which those attacks are only a reflective part. Yet for Waldrop the fact of the towers' collapse exceeds representation because its constant loop on television exchanges the historical-political specificity of the event for an 'image on a screen.'[3] It is simply one image among others:

> Like a movie. Like a comic strip. Please distinguish between. Crumbling towers and the image of crumbling towers. The image, repeated, multiplies. Locks on the plural. Crowds.[4]

Waldrop's aesthetic is driven by two main aims. First, the appeal to distinction is motivated by a concern for accuracy. In this sense, Waldrop's appeal is motivated by a concern for the incomprehensible

---

[1] Waldrop, 'Disaster,' *Love, Like Pronouns* (Richmond, CA: Omnidawn, 2003) p.116.
[2] ibid, pp.113-114.
[3] ibid, p.115.
[4] ibid, p.113.

itself. That the singular fact of the event not be reduced, which is to say, that it not be repeatable, it is necessary, Waldrop suggests, to maintain a distance between the event and its representation. In this way, and second, in the absence of any clear specificity the event's media repetition becomes indivisible from the event's concealment. The unique quality of the event, in other words, actually gets lost because its constant media repetition renders it excessively transparent. As the opening lines of 'Disaster' illustratively put it:

> Went and looked and went and looked. For what was no more. Scrutinized screens and saw. Nothing. The papers in the land and. Took in nothing.[5]

Or again, at the beginning of the fourth section: 'nothing is hidden. Therefore cannot see. Therefore a view of the world unimportant.'[6]

Waldrop turns this sense of 'nothing' into a critical project. It is, Waldrop puts it, a nothing that 'has room. For all. No ruins can fill it. No rubble. No number of dead.'[7] From this perspective, the 'nothing' Waldrop proposes is both the distillation and the consequence of the events of September 11, 2001. More specifically, it is the representation of those events *as disaster*. By not only clearing but also maintaining a space into which the events of September 11 disappear, 'nothing' paradoxically renders tangible the events of that day. Waldrop emphasises what is at stake here at the start of the second section when she writes that '[a] hole is. A space for thought.'[8] It is more than probable that the noun 'space' in this passage refers less to 'thought' than it does to the interruptive mark of the full stop point that both precedes and typifies it. As with paradox, then, such syntax works by both prohibiting and suggesting representation. Nothing is conferred upon 'a hole' beyond the basic statement of its existence—'a hole is.' In other words, it becomes legible precisely because the poem derives nothing from it. Hence, even as the existence of a 'hole' may well be contiguous with 'a space for thought,' and vice versa, neither, in fact, is continuous with the other. Indeed, Waldrop develops this inter-relation between contiguity and fissure in the following lines from the third section:

---

[5] ibid, p.113.
[6] ibid, p.116.
[7] ibid, p.113.
[8] ibid, p.114.

> Often we must work with holes. In understanding. Often set out without knowing where. Often distrust narratives.[9]

It is this sense of prohibition against representation that conditions Waldrop's sense of 'disaster'. In other words, 'Disaster' is understood to signify the looped tension between effacement and remainder. Maurice Blanchot helps illustrate what is at stake in such a definition when he writes that 'the disaster ruins everything, all the while leaving everything intact.'[10] It performs this strange double act, Blanchot goes on to suggest, because the disaster itself is properly unthinkable; it is unpronounceable and illegible. In part, this is the case because, taken literally, disaster would signify the ruin of discourse. But there is also another sense of disaster which plays a pivotal role in the development of Waldrop's point in this poem. 'Disaster,' Blanchot states, 'means being separated from the star;' dés-astre: 'break with the star, break with every form of totality.'[11] In other words, disaster intends that which is without reference. It communicates not by bringing together but by setting apart. As such, what the disaster communicates hardly matters. What is of concern, rather, is the line it draws through whatever it is that comes to be said; what matters is its prohibition against reference. In relation to Waldrop's poem, the key point is that 'disaster' directs the sequence from the perspective of what it has not been quite possible to say. The gaps in the poem's narrative are crucial. Each break in the narrative becomes a mark of omission, a mark of a word inferred but not recorded.

For Waldrop, then, the political is to be thought from the threshold of definability, at that point where conceptualisation opens itself to frequent revision. As Giorgio Agamben notes, in various European languages the notion of the 'outside' is expressed:

> by a word that means 'at the door' (*fores* in Latin is the door of the house, *thyrathen* in Greek literally means 'at the threshold'). The *outside* is not another space that resides beyond a determinate space, but rather, it is the passage, the exteriority that gives it access—in a world, it is its face, its *eidos*.[12]

---

[9] ibid, p.115.
[10] Maurice Blanchot, *The Writing of the Disaster*, p. 1.
[11] ibid, p.2, and p. 75.
[12] Giorgio Agamben, *The Coming Community*, trans. Michael Hardt (Minneapolis and London: University of Minnesota Press, 2005) p.67.

The error, Waldrop notes, is to attempt to fill the space of openness (from which all relationality emerges) 'with flags. [...] When a foreign language we should be required to learn.'[13] In this respect, the Bush administration's mobilisation of a predominantly symbolic solidarity premised on the exaggeration of national allegiance (of which the flying of flags would be one example) that followed—and that continues to be secured against—the attacks in New York and Washington would appear to inform the trajectory of Waldrop's intervention.

If the form of prohibition and reticence that structures 'Disaster' has a political force, it concerns an imperative to be open towards foreignness. Kimberley Lamm reads Waldrop's understanding of foreignness in relation to Deleuze and Guattari's sense of minor literature, specifically the sensation or experience of being a 'foreigner in one's own language.' For Lamm, such foreignness enables Waldrop 'to see, break up, imagine, and revise historical texts and in constructions of the self and personhood traced and retraced by history and habit.' As Lamm continues, 'between the texture of a life lived and a text on the page, there are spaces of translation—lines of flight and escape—that reconfigure the already imagined shape of the self, that even demolish the precedence of a self.' For Deleuze and Guattari, Lamm goes on to explain, these 'lines of flight' are:

> resistant and desiring formations of movement engaged in the process of deterritorialization, movements of 'becoming' engaged in the process of interrupting orders of thought, breaking cemented maps that leads to the mirrored ends of familiar ideas and historical memories. A line of flight is the appearance of a 'heterogeneous line.' A line of flight does not move toward 'freedom'—a state enforced by dominant circumscription—but becomes new paths that don't already exist.[14]

As Deleuze and Guattari put it, 'the problem is not that of being free but of finding a way out, or even a way in, another side, a hallway, an adjacency.'[15]

---

[13] Waldrop, 'Disaster,' p.114.
[14] Kimberley Lamm, 'Gender in a Minor Key: Rosmarie Waldrop's *A Key into the Language of America*,' *How2*, Vol. 1, No. 8 (Fall 2002), http://www.asu.edu/pipercwcenter/how2journal/archive/online_archive/v1_8_2002/current/readings/lamm.htm, accessed 7 August 2012.
[15] Gilles Deleuze and Felix Guattari, *Kafka: Toward a Minor Literature*, trans.

'We must write poetry,' Waldrop comments in interview, 'because we must pay attention to language because it constitutes our identity as human beings. But we must write with "wounded words." We must be aware of—and responsive to—the horrors as well as the beauties. We must not sequester ourselves.'[16] 'Our language,' Waldrop writes elsewhere, 'defines us.'[17]

> I've often said that poets are a kind of 'maintenance crew' for language, making sure it can function properly. But it would always be a small, particular area you work on [...] So you make some small structures that use language as precisely and imaginatively as you can—and hope it will make a little counterweight against politicians' spin and the daily 'transparent' use.[18]

Waldrop quotes Robert Oppenheimer's caution against political attempts at synthesis: 'We are condemned to live in a world where every question opens another, and that to infinity [...] I am afraid that all those who still aspire to synthesis or unity are wishfully calling for a time that is past. I am afraid they will obtain this synthesis only at the price of either tyranny or renunciation.'[19]

For Emily Carr, Waldrop's work is political precisely because it is 'in-between'; it is political, Carr notes, 'primarily in the sense of its playfulness, its intoxication with the failure of closure, its attempt to subvert authority through both quotation and misquotation, and its investment in the fertile ground between dichotomies.'[20] 'It is sometimes forgotten,' writes the poet Michael Palmer:

> that there is a profoundly historical and social dimension to such hermetic speech, that is its own form of intervention, and that its resistance to meaning [...] is shared by many types of poetry, including some of the most avowedly public and/or 'transparent.' Before the contradictions and paradoxes

---

Dana Polan (Minneapolis and London: University of Minnesota Press, 1986) p.8.
[16] Cooperman, 'Between Tongues.'
[17] Waldrop, *Lavish Absence*, p.59.
[18] Email to author, 27 August 2006.
[19] Robert Oppenheimer, interview with Dr Escoffier-Lambiotte, Le Monde, 29 April, 1958; quoted in Lavish Absence, p.35.
[20] Emily Carr, 'Happily, Revision: Reading Rosmarie Waldrop's *The Reproduction of Profiles*, Jacket 36 (Late 2008), para. 7, http://jacketmagazine.com/36/r-waldrop-rb-carr-emily.shtml, accessed 5 December 2011.

of the real, including the quotidian, those very paradoxes and contradictions become agents of articulation and the reassertion of meaning.[21]

Waldrop: 'Poetry, like philosophy, leaves everything as it is. But in spite of this, when your government consistently lies through its teeth, it just may be very important to pay attention to words in the way poetry does.'[22]

To theorise the political in terms of lamentation or refusal is neither to withdraw nor to relegate the event of political life. Read from the perspective of refusal, lamentation not only represents the politics of today but, crucially, it does so in the fragile dispersal of its structure, by putting into question its very own relevance. Lamentation trembles precariously at the edge of life, an interplay of falling and forming. Maurice Blanchot calls refusal a 'power' but he does so not because refusal acts productively in the world, but because its mute gesture introduces a structural rift into political economy. 'When we refuse,' Blanchot writes, 'we refuse with a movement that is without contempt, without exaltation, and anonymous, as far as possible, for the power to refuse cannot come from us, not in our name alone, but from a very poor beginning that belongs first to those who cannot speak.'[23] And besides, as Derrida cautions: '[a]s soon as one identifies a revolution, it begins to imitate, it enters into a death agony.'[24]

Thus Waldrop can note how 'our inclusive views are mosaics. And the shards catch light on the cut, [and] the edges give off sparks.'[25] They do so, perhaps, as a kind of abstraction, and as catastrophe is to emergence.

---

[21] Michael Palmer, 'Active Boundaries,' pp.213-4.
[22] Cooperman, 'Between Tongues.'
[23] Maurice Blanchot, 'Refusal,' *Friendship*, p. 112.
[24] Jacques Derrida, *Specters of Marx: State of the Debt, The Work of Mourning, and The New International*, trans. Peggy Kamuf (London and New York: Routledge, 1994) p. 115.
[25] Waldrop, *Ceci*, p. 86.

'Something Else Than a Stretch of Earth': Living in America

In the introduction to her 1994 work, *A Key into the Language of America*, Waldrop writes:

> I live in the former territory of the Narragansett Indians, in Rhode Island, the colony Williams founded as a haven of religious freedom after he was banished from the theocratic Massachusetts Bay Colony for his nonconformist opinions. I was not born here. Like the first settlers, I came from Europe. I came expecting strangeness, expecting to be disorientated, but was shocked, rather, by my lack of culture shock.[1]

What did strike Waldrop as unfamiliar, though, were the numerous Indian place names.

> I was at first irritated by them: my ears could not take them in, my eyes were disorientated by their spelling [...] Then, gradually, I became fascinated with the irritant, the otherness of these names, the strangeness of their music, which alone inscribes the Indian past in the present space. The Narragansett language, not written down, existed only in time and vanished with it.[2]

In order to understand something of the cultural and geographical history of the local area, Waldrop turned to the 17th century work, *A Key into the Language of America*, by Roger Williams. Published in 1643 Williams' book is, first and foremost, a phrasebook and study of the Narragansett language, but it is also an ethnographic study of Indian customs and a record of Williams' own personal encounter with what he experienced as 'otherness'. The anthropological research that went into the compiling of Williams' *A Key* was premised as much on bearing witness to the glory of God as it was on the ethnographic preservation of an Indian language, but it was also premised on Williams' preparedness to open himself to separateness. It is a field report that, at least implicitly, also worked to dispel the myth of virgin land and the legitimacy of royal charters.

---

[1] Rosmarie Waldrop, 'A Key into the Key,' p.188.
[2] ibid, pp.188-189.

Lodging with the Narragansett tribe and learning their language well enough that he could debate with them in their own tongue, Williams hoped that *A Key* would also turn out to be 'the little *Key*' that paved the way for David's 'bunch of Keyes', which opened the door to the kingdom of Heaven. 'A little key,' he writes, 'may open a box, where lies a bunch of keys.' Or as Williams writes at the end of *A Key*, 'I have had such converse with Barbarous Nations, and have been mercifully assisted, to frame this poore KEY, which may, (through His Blessing) in His owne holy season open a Doore: yea, Doors of unknowne Mercies to Us and Them, be Honour, Glory, Power, Riches, Wisdome, Goodnesse and Dominion ascribed by all His in Jesus Christ to Eternity, Amen.'[3]

For Waldrop, it was Williams' interweaving of lexical documentation and a personally mediated engagement with cultural difference that interested her most. 'I was born in 1935,' Waldrop reminds readers, the same year:

> Williams' 300-year banishment officially ended. I was born 'on the other side,' in Germany. Which was the Nazi Germany. I am not Jewish. I was born on the side of the (then) winners. I was still a child when World War II ended with the defeat of the Nazis. I immigrated to the U.S., the country of the winners, as a white, educated European who did not find it too difficult to get jobs, an advanced degree, a university position. I can see myself, to some extent, as a parallel to the European settlers/colonists of Roger Williams' time (though I did not think God or destiny had set aside for me a virgin garden). Like Roger Williams, I am ambivalent about my position among the privileged, the 'conquerors'.[4]

As Steve Evans has commented, in Williams:

> Waldrop finds a fascinatingly contradictory anchor point for a sustained meditation on her adopted country. Exile and translator, a figure of radical independence (to the point of being labeled a heretic), Williams was a man whose prototypical act of sympathetic anthropology slipped into an appalling and unsought complicity with the process of colonization. The

---

[3] Roger Williams, *The Complete Writings of Roger Williams, Vol.1*, ed. Edwin Gaustad (New York, Russell and Russell, 2007) p.279.
[4] Waldrop, 'A Key into the Key,' p.192.

ubiquity of Williams' image and name in modern-day Rhode Island, where she makes her home, leads Waldrop to say in the extremely useful introduction to the *Key*: 'I live in Roger Williams' territory. By coincidence and marriage I share his initials. I share his ambivalence.'[5]

Here, and across her work, political opening and the experience of margins are intertwined by Waldrop, brought together in layers and folds. Waldrop's *A Key into the Language of America* extends Waldrop's engagement with the conquest of the Americas and America's early colonial history, as well as the juxtaposed relationships between conquering and exploring, discovery and foreignness, which she had begun in *Shorter American Memory* (1988) and the cross-genre work, *A Form/of Taking/It All*, written between 1983 and 1985, but not published until 1990. 'The limits of this field can never be exactly known,' Waldrop writes in the fragmentary sequence which closes *A Form*. 'Only the discovery that certain phenomena can no longer be ordered by means of the old concepts tells us that we have reached the limit.'[6]

> the images break on the shore
> images and expectations
> the window
> and the frame of understanding
> whatever
> swims out of view
> you
> do not match my interpretations[7]

As Joan Retallack notes in conversation with Waldrop, 'this is really about the way, the only way, we can experience history, dispersed as it is in the particles we move through in the everyday life of the present, taking things in according to the particulars of our associative networks of our cultural and personal moment.'[8] Commenting on the implications of Waldrop's poetic method in these works, Johanna Drucker notes how there is what she describes as a:

---

[5] Evans, 'Rosmarie Waldrop.'
[6] Rosmarie Waldrop, *A Form/of Taking/It All* (Evanston, IL: Northwestern University Press, 2001) p.245.
[7] ibid, p.239.
[8] Retallack, 'A Conversation between Joan Retallack and Rosmarie Waldrop, Pt.2.'

sensitivity to the cultural history of language and to the historical significances [...] of these documents that have this incredible public impact. So I think part of what we see here is how her encounter with American poetics and American linguistic formations is part of what she's engaged with, and I think it's also the outsider's test of understanding. In other words, I think I know what this means but I know it in translation. So if I do this kind of a translation, then what do I know about what I know? And what does that say back to those of you who know this document in what you think is the original? Because the original, of course, comes to us across a great distance of space and time, and encodes its own cultural history.[9]

Thus when Waldrop subsequently turned to Roger Williams' *A Key into the Language of America* as the source text for her next project, it was largely with a view to developing the poetic theme and method of cultural exploration and translation.

Each of the thirty-two chapters of Williams' *A Key into the Language of America* consists of three stages: vocabulary and lists of phrases, anthropological observations, and a final moralising poem. Here is an abbreviated version of Chapter XVIII , Of the Sea:

Echêkum. | *The Sea*
Kítthan | *The Sea-God*, or, that name which they give that Deitie or Godhead which they conceive to be in the sea.
    Obs. Mishoòn an *Indian* Boat, or Canow made of Pine or Oake, or Chestnut-tree: I have seene a Native goe into the woods with his hatchet, carrying onely a Basket of Corne with him, & stones to strike fire when he had feld his tree (being a *chesnut*) he made him a little House or shed of the bark of it, he puts fire and followes the burning of it with fire, in the midst in many places: his corne he boyles and hath the Brook by him, and sometimes angles for a little fish; but so hee continues burning and hewing untill he hath within ten or twelve dayes (lying there at his worke alone) finished, and (getting hands,) lanched his Boate; with which afterward hee ventures out to

---

[9] Johanna Drucker, 'Inalienable Writes: Rosmarie Waldrop, "Shorter American Memory of the Declaration of Independence,"' *Poem Talk*, *#47*, 10 November 2011, https://jacket2.org/commentary/inalienable-writes-poemtalk-47, accessed 6 August 2012.

fish in the Ocean.
Mishoonémese. | A little Canow.
    Some of them will not well carry above three or foure: but some of them twenty, thirty, forty men.
Wunnauanoúnuck. | A Shallop.
Wunnauanounuckquèse. | A Skiffe.
    Obs. Although themselves have neither, yet they give them such names, which in their Language signifieth carrying Vessels.

[...]

They see Gods wonders that are call'd
   Through dreadfull Seas to passe,
In tearing winds and roaring seas,
   And calmes as smooth as glasse.
I have in Europes *ships, oft been*
   In King of terrours hand;
When all have cri'd, Now, now we sinck,
   Yet God bronght safe to land.
Alone 'mongst Indians *in Canoes,*
   Sometimes o're-turn'd, I have been
Halfe inch from death, in Ocean deepe,
   Gods wonders I have seene.[10]

Waldrop's book also comprises 32 sections and largely follows Williams' pattern and structure, but adds a fourth strand. The initial sections in prose parallel Williams' anthropological commentary relating to the 'clash' of cultures. This is followed by a list of words partially drawn from Williams' text and partly derived from Waldrop's own Western heritage. Each word list is then followed by an italicised section that weaves first-person fragments together about a young woman ambivalent about both her gender and her position among the 'conquerors'. The final element comprises a short poem that reframes phrases from earlier sections of the book by changing their context and splicing them with new material. It is a poetic process that works by degrees. 'I try,' Waldrop adds, 'to enact the confrontation of the two cultures by juxtapositions, often within a single sentence.'[11] As Waldrop

---
[10] Roger Williams, *A Key into the Language of America* (Bedford, MA: Applewood Books, 1997) pp.106-111.
[11] Waldrop, 'A Key into the Key,' p.194.

goes on to add:

> The words in the lists may be suggested by the sound of a title word (e.g., 'fission' in the chapter on fishing) or may play across its semantic field ('interlacing' and 'contagion' in the chapter on 'Relations of Consanguinity'). Many lists explore compounds of title words (busy[body], [body]guard, [body] snatcher in Chapter 7) or grammatical elements like suffixes ([season]able, [season]ing in Chapter 10). There are also some Narragansett phrases.[12]

In relation to this method, then, in Waldrop's book the section 'Of the Sea' becomes:

> A site of passage, of dreadful to move on, of depth between. A native **will take his hatchet** to the Latin of daily life (without postulating long neighbourhood or early development) **and burn hew until he has launched** his morphological innovation on the water. Great transport of bodies, some carrying thirty, forty men.
>
> [...]
>
>   bed
>   biscuit
>   cucumber
>   farer
>   mstress
>   nce
>   scape
>   son
>
> *Against the threat of frigidity, I sought out thermal cures which brought me contact with short hair, gratitude, parts called private and more or less so. Without these unidentical skins, masts might have snapped and left me lying right underneath the sky. But my flesh close up was pale and terrified my lover.*
>
>   a verb
>   tense beyond
>   my innermost dark thoughts
>   but holds

---

[12] ibid, p.195.

>   no water
>   no more than swimmers see
>   beyond displacement
>   in exchange[13]

Waldrop's process here should not be confused with pastiche or parody; nor is it procedural. Rather, in various ways Waldrop's version of *A Key* might be understood as a kind of textual and cultural recovery. And even though Williams' text may well provide Waldrop with both the spur and the source, her work is largely a textual and cultural recovery of a very personal sense of foreignness. 'All in all,' Waldrop writes, 'my book could be called an immigrant's take on the heritage and complex early history of my adopted country.'[14] At the same time, Waldrop's book becomes a means to map out a discourse of lost origins. In his essay, 'Pressures of Never-at-home,' Vincent Broqua reads Waldrop's text as calling into question any notion of a 'language of America' and the sense of hegemony any such definition wold imply. For Roger Williams, Broqua writes, the language of 'America' is:

> a foreign tongue, a language that he wishes the settlers to learn so as to be able to understand and live with a foreign yet native population. For Waldrop, the language of America is both the natives' and American English. Seen from her linguistic 'non place', America and its language are forever under Waldrop's poetic scrutiny. Because of her ambivalent position, she never envisages language as a transparent and familiar medium to the poet.[15]

As Broqua continues:

> In *A Key*, a clearly delimited space is being estranged into sites whose stability is jeopardised. The fluctuations and displacements that these *differentiating sites of passage* create allow Waldrop to question her estranged and estranging identity as writer and reader.[16]

---

[13] ibid, pp.37-38.
[14] ibid, p.195.
[15] Vincent Broqua, 'Pressures of Never-at-Home,' *Jacket* 32 (April 2007), para. 15, http://jacketmagazine.com/32/p-broqua.shtml, accessed 5 December 2011.
[16] ibid, para. 20.

'The enormous migration from Europe to America, wave after wave of explorers, conquerors, immigrants. Being part of this,' Waldrop writes, 'has marked me. It was my third change of world. It surfaces again and again in my writing.'[17]

As with the relation between poetry and politics, it is for these reasons that Kimberley Lamm has noted the ways in which Waldrop's text mirrors Deleuze's and Guattari's sense of a 'minor literature,' which is to say a literature which deterritorialises language, that takes place on the margins but in so doing destabilises the centre, 'that which a minority constructs within a major language.'[18] For Lamm, Waldrop's text both reflects and complicates this theory. The 'movement away from sense and subjectivity,' Lamm writes, 'is rare in *A Key into the Language of America*, since the history the young woman finds herself within enforces impediment to every line of flight by denying her a glimpse of recognition or coherence.'[19] This is the alternate, and sometime simultaneous push and pull that plays out across so much of Waldrop's writing, the paradox between quantum and wave; the cuff between flow and fragmentation, prose and poetry.

Geography, movement, shift, language, migration, change, flux; a writing caught on the bluff; the politics of place and home, of selfhood, are interwoven in different ways throughout each of Waldrop's texts. Hers is a poetry that melds history, archival research, lexicography, cartography, speculation, biography, chance, time spent looking out the window, and it does so most specifically, most vitally, at the level of spindle, form. As Waldrop comments of her 1990 novel, *A Form/ Of Taking/ It All*, she is engaged in an 'exploration of otherness', of all that cannot be folded back into the same; otherness as place, as language, history, home; as point of relation; as way of life.[20] Much of the time, most of the world's folds are a personal topography.

---

[17] Waldrop, 'Between, Always,' p.272
[18] Deleuze and Guattari, *Kafka: Toward a Minor Literature*, p.16.
[19] Kimberley Lamm, 'Gender in a Minor Key: Rosmarie Waldrop's *A Key into the Language of America*.'
[20] Retallack, 'A Conversation,' p.372.

Bluff

In Waldrop's most recent book, *Driven to Abstraction*, the first section of the first sequence, 'All Electrons Are (Not) Alike,' reads:

> A view of the sea is the beginning of the journey. An image of Columbus, starting out from the abyss, enters the left hemisphere. Profusion of languages out of the blue. Bluster, blur, blubber. My father was disturbed by inklings of Babel and multiplication on his table. Afraid that an overload of simultaneous neural firings would result in an epileptic convulsion. The explorers' attention, like the foot of a snail, held on to the planks of their vessels, not communicating. Too intent on the physical fact, waves, whales, or poison arrows. Later, though, poured forth stories never dreamed of by the natives. As if languages were kidnapped as easily as green shady land profuse of flowers.[1]

Surfaces can be difficult to read and the slate is never wiped clean, really, no matter the scourer used. Lines of reference are tangled, an entire condensed pattern of connection. Driven to abstraction. Besides, it is not always easy to be what one says; matter lost in grammar and convention, and convergence too the edge of letting go.

To move in the spaces language opens.

A place where life and writing come together; an engagement with history, ground, that is also a way of thinking the rifts of life, its relative strangeness, the stuff of things, some of it choppier than the rest; a whole made up of pieces, fragments: the gaps, the inconsistencies, the blindsights. Most often, contradictions are restless and ambiguity pulls in more than one direction.

* * *

> *bluff, n., a cliff or headland with a broad precipitous face. (First used in North America, and still mostly of American landscapes)*

* * *

---

[1] Rosmarie Waldrop, *Driven to Abstraction* (New York: New Directions, 2010) p.5.

In 1900 Max Planck found that energy emission and absorption took place not smoothly and continuously as dictated by a view of nature inherited by Newton and Maxwell, but discontinuously, in pulses or packets of energy: that is, in discrete measurable units or 'quanta'.

According to the third law of thermodynamics, developed between 1906 and 1912 by the German physicist, Walter Nernst, absolute zero is the point at which no more heat can be extracted from a system. For Nernst, a system at absolute zero temperature exists only in its ground state, where a ground state is to be understood as the lowest possible energy a physical system may have: its zero-point energy.

* * *

> 'And when the name, blessed be He, wanted to create the world, there was no room to create it, because everything was infinite. Because of this, He contracted the "light" toward the sides and by means of this withdrawal an "empty space" was formed. And inside this "empty space" the days and measures came into existence that constituted the major part of the creation of the world.
>
> This "empty space" was logically necessary to allow the creation of the world. For without this "empty space", there would have been no room for the creation of the world as we have just said.'[2]

Discoveries in modern science tell us the universe is expanding. Perhaps there is no great difference of opinion here. Having been formed, the world, now, stretches back to its beginnings.

* * *

In interview, Waldrop comments how continuities, smooth transitions, tend to be false. The sense that one thing follows on from another is bluff, an illusion of order. 'There is always,' she says, 'the feeling that I never have enough information. The process is not so much "telling" as questioning. This implies interruption. And in the gaps we might

---

[2] Ouaknin, *The Burnt Book*, p.269.

get hints of much that has to be left unsaid—but should be thought about.'[3]

* * *

'Pulling pieces of geometry, geology, alchemy, philosophy, politics, biography, biology, mythology, and philology from alien territory, a [...] woman audaciously invented a new grammar grounded in humility and hesitation. HESITATE from the Latin, meaning to stick. Stammer. To hold back in doubt, have difficulty speaking.'[4]

> *essay, n. from the French, essai, to weigh, try, measure, inquire into; a rough copy; first draft.*

'to seek to receive the other as other and the foreign as foreign; to seek *autrui*, therefore, in [...] irreducible difference, in [...] infinite strangeness, an empty strangeness, and such that only an essential discontinuity can retain the affirmation proper to it [...] And this means therefore: not fearing to affirm interruption and rupture in order to come to the point of proposing and expressing—an infinite task—a truly plural speech.'[5]

'To carry from one place to another. To continue thinking, to think from another place, another perspective.' 'Myself a different person.'[6]

---

[3] Retallack, 'A Conversation,' p.341.
[4] Susan Howe, *My Emily Dickinson* (New York: New Directions, 2007) p.21.
[5] Blanchot, *The Infinite Conversation*, p.82.
[6] Waldrop, *Lavish Absence*, p.149.

Bibliography

Adorno, Theodor, *Minima Moralia: Reflections from Damaged Life*, trans. E.F.N. Jephcott (London: Verso, 1978).

Adorno, Theodor, *Aesthetic Theory*, trans. Robert Hullot-Kentor (Minneapolis: University of Minnesota Press, 1997).

Adorno, Theodor, *Critical Models*, trans. Henry W. Pickford (New York: Columbia University Press, 1998).

Agamben, Giorgio, *Means Without End*, trans. Vincenzo Binetti and Cesare Casarino (Minneapolis: University of Minnesota Press, 2000).

Agamben, Giorgio, *The Coming Community*, trans. Michael Hardt (Minneapolis and London: University of Minnesotta Press, 2005).

Andrews, Bruce, and Charles Bernstein (eds.), *The L=A=N=G=U=A=G=E Book* (Carbondale and Edwardsville: Southern Illinois University Press, 1984).

Antin, David, '"Some Questions about Modernism," *Occident*, 8 (Spring 1974), pp.7-38.

Ashbery, John, *A Conversation with Kenneth Koch* (New York: Interview Press, 1965).

Axelrod, Steven Gould et al. (eds.), *Modernisms: 1900-1950, Vol.2* (New Brunswick, NJ: Rutgers University Press, 2007).

Bachelard, Gaton, *The Poetics of Space* (Boston, MA: Beacon Press, 1994).

Bakhtin, Mikhail, *Problems of Dostoyevsky's Poetics* (University of Minnesota Press, 1984).

Barbato, Joseph, 'On the Edge with Burning Deck', *Publisher's Weekly*, Vol. 237, No.33 (1990) pp.40-41.

Bassoff, Bruce, 'Gertrude Stein's "Composition as Explanation,"' *Twentieth Century Literature*, Vol. 24, No.1 (Spring, 1978) pp.76-80.

Bataille, Georges, *My Mother, Madame Edwarda, The Dead Man*, trans. Austryn Wainhouse (London and New York: Marion Boyars, 1995).

Beach, Christopher, *Poetic Culture: Contemporary American Poetry Between Community and Institution* (Evanston, IL: Northwestern University Press, 1999).

Beckett, Samuel, *Disjecta: Miscellaneous Writings and a Dramatic Fragment*, ed. Ruby Cohn (London: John Calder, 1983).

Bénézet, Mathieu, 'Claude Royet-Journoud Interviewed,' *Shearsman*, No. 2 (1981) pp.56-58.

Benjamin, Walter, *Illuminations: Essays and Reflections*, ed. Hannah Arendt (New York: Schocken Books, 1968).

Benjamin, Walter, *Selected Writings, 1931-1934*, ed. Michael William Jennings (Cambridge, MA: Harvard University Press, 2005).

Benjamin, Walter, *One Way Street and Other Writings*, trans. J.A. Underwood (London: Penguin, 2009).

Bernstein, Charles (ed.), *The Politics of Poetic Form: Poetry and Public Policy* (New York: Roof Books, 1990).
Bernstein, Charles, *My Way: Speeches and Poems* (Chicago: The University of Chicago Press, 1999).
Binkiewicz, Donna M., *Federalizing the Muse: United States Art Policy and the National Endowment for the Arts 1965-1980* (The University of North Carolina Press, 2004).
Blanchot, Maurice, *L'Entretien Infini* (Paris: Gallimard, 1971).
Blanchot, *The Space of Literature*, trans. Ann Smock (Lincoln and London: University of Nebraska Press, 1982).
Blanchot, Maurice, *Vicious Circles: Two Fictions and After the Fact*, trans. Paul Auster (Barrytown, NY: Station Hill Press, 1985).
Blanchot, Maurice, *The Step Not Beyond*, trans. Lycette Nelson (Albany, NY: State University of New York Press, 1992).
Blanchot, Maurice, *The Infinite Conversation*, trans. Susan Hanson (Minneapolis and London: University of Minnesota Press, 1993).
Blanchot, Maurice, *The Work of Fire*, trans. Charlotte Mandell (Stanford, CA: Stanford University Press, 1995).
Blanchot, Maurice, *The Writing of the Disaster*, trans. Ann Smock (Lincoln and London: University of Nebsraska Press, 1995).
Blanchot, Maurice, *Friendship*, trans. Elizabeth Rottenberg (Stanford, CA: Stanford University Press, 1997).
Borradori, Giovanna (ed.), *Philosophy in a Time of Terror* (Chicago and London: The University of Chicago Press).
Brecht, Stefan, *The Original Theatre of the City of New York: From the Mid 60s to the Mid 70s, Book 1, The Theatre of Visions: Robert Wilson* (Frankfurt: Suhrkamp Verlag, 1978).
Broqua, Vincent, 'Pressures 'Pressures of Never-at-home,' *Jacket* 32 (April, 2007), http://jacketmagazine/32/p-broqua.shtml.
Bruns, Gerald L., *Heidegger's Estrangements: Language, Truth and Poetry* (New Haven: Yale University Press, 1989).
Buck-Morris, Susan, *The Dialectics of Seeing: Walter Benjamin and the Arcades Project* (Cambridge, MA: MIT Press, 1991).
Buckley, Paul and F. David Peat, *Glimpsing Reality: Ideas in Physics and the Link to Biology* (Toronto: University of Toronto Press, 1996).
Cage, John, 'Nicholas Zurbrugg Interviews John Cage,' *Eyeline*, No. 1 (May, 1987).
Carr, Emily, 'Happily, Revision: Reading Rosmarie Waldrop's *The Reproduction of Profiles*,' *Jacket*, 36 (Late 2008), http://jacketmagazine.com/36/r-waldrop-rb-carr-emily.shtml.
Cicero, *De inventione, De optimo genere oratorum, topica*, trans. H.M. Hubbell (Cambridge, MA: Harvard University Press. 1960).
Clark, Timothy, *Martin Heidegger* (London: Routledge, 2002).

Cole, Norma, *Crosscut Universe: Writing on Writing From France* (Providence: Burning Deck, 2000).

Cooperman, Matthew, 'Between Tongues: An Interview with Rosmarie Waldrop,' *Conjunctions* (2005), http://www.conjunctions.com/webcon/cooperman.htm.

Craig, Blanche (ed.), *Collage: Assembling Contemporary Art* (London: Black Dog Publishing, 2008).

Critchley, Simon, 'Tom McCarthy and Simon Critchley in conversation: Beckett, Adorno, Blanchot, Comedy, Death, and so on….,' *Office of Anti-Matter*, Austrian Cultural Institute, London (29 March 2001), http://voidmanufacturing.wordpress.com/2008/12/09/tom-mccarthy-and-simon-critchley-in-conversation-beckett-adorno-blanchot-comedy-death-and-so-on.

Cuno, James (ed.), *Foirades/Fizzles: Echo and Allusion in the Art of Jasper Johns* (Los Angeles: The Grunewald Center for the Graphic Arts and Wight Art Gallery at UCLA, 1987).

Deleuze, Gilles, *Essays Critical and Clinical*, trans. Daniel W. Smith and Michael A. Greco (London and New York: Verso, 1998).

Deleuze, Gilles and Felix Guattari, *Kafka: Toward a Minor Literature*, trans. Dana Polan (Minneapolis and London: University of Minnesota Press, 1986).

Demick, Jared, 'An Interview with Keith and Rosmarie Waldrop,' *The Jivin' Ladybug*, http://mysite.verizon.net/vze8911e/jivinladybug/id53.html.

Denut, Eric, 'Interview with Charles Bernstein,' *The Argotist Online*, http://www.argotistonline.co.uk/Bernstein%20interview.htm.

Derrida, Jacques, *Margins of Philosophy*, trans. Alan Bass (Chicago and London: University of Chicago Press, 1982).

Derrida, Jacques, *Specters of Marx: State of the Debt, The Work of Mourning, and The New International*, trans. Peggy Kamuf (London and New York: Routledge, 1994).

Derrida, Jacques, 'Edmond Jabès and the Question of the Book,' *Writing and Difference*, trans. Alan Bass (London: Routledge, 2001) pp.77-96.

Derrida, Jacques, *Acts of Religion* (ed. Gil Anidjar), (London and New York: Routledge, 2002).

Drob, Stanford L., 'Jacques Derrida and the Kabbalah,' *The New Kabbalah* (2006), http://www.newkabbalah.com/JDK.pdf.

Drucker, Johanna, 'Inalienable Writes: Rosmarie Waldrop, "Shorter American Memory of the Declaration of Independence,"' Poem Talk, #47, 10 November 2011, https://jacket2.org/commentary/inalienable-writes-poemtalk-47.

Dunn, Richard S., and Laetitia Yeandle (eds.), *The Journal of John Winthrop, 1630-1649* (Cambridge, MA: Harvard University Press, 1996).

Duffy, Nikolai, 'The Poetics of Emergency', *Jacket*, 32 (April, 2007), http://jacketmagazine.com/32/p-duffy.shtml.

Egerton, Michael Tod, 'This Half-Life Explicated by Touch: On Two Recent Books by Burning Deck Press', *Jacket*, 40 (Late 2010), http://jacketmagazine.com/40/edgerton-on-the-burning-deck.shtml.

Evans, Steve, 'Rosmarie Waldrop,' *Dictionary of Literary Biography, vol. 169: American Poets Since WWII* (Stamford, CT: Gale, 1998); reprinted at: *Third Fiction Factory: Notes to Poetry* (2006), www.thirdfactory.net/archive_waldrop.html.

Fenollosa, Ernest, *The Chinese Written Character as a Medium for Poetry* (San Francisco: City Lights, 1964).

Foster, Edward, *Postmodern Poetry: The Talisman Interviews* (Hoboken, NJ: Talisman House, 1994).

Franklin, Wayne, *The Norton Anthology of American Literature, Vol. A*, 8th edition (New York and London: Norton, 2012).

Freitag, Kornelia, *Cultural Criticism in Women's Experimental Writing: The Poetry of Rosmarie Waldrop, Lyn Hejinian and Susan Howe* (Heidelberg: Universitätsverlag, 2006).

Freitag, Kornelia, and Katharina Vester (eds.), *Another Language: Poetic Experiments in Britain and North America* (Münster, Lit Verlag, 2008).

Gander, Forrest, *A Faithful Existence: Reading, Memory, Transcendence* (Denver, CO: Counterpoint Press, 2005).

Gavronsky, Serge, *Towards a New Poetics: Contemporary Writing in France* (Berkeley, CA: University of California Press, 1994).

Gentzler, Edwin, *Contemporary Translation Theories* (Clevedon: Multilingual Matters, 2001).

Gould, Eric (ed.), *The Sin of the Book*, (Lincoln: University of Nebraska Press, 1985).

Graham, J.F. (ed.), *Difference in Translation* (Ithaca, NY: Cornell University Press, 1985).

Hallberg, Robert van, 'Olson, Whitehead, and the Objectivists,' *Boundary 2*, Vol. 2, Nos.1-2 (1973-1974), pp.85-112.

Hamilton-Emery, Chris, *101 Ways to Make Poems Sell: The Salt Guide to Getting and Staying Published* (Cambridge: Salt Publishing, 2006).

Harbach, Chad, 'MFA vs. NYC', *Slate Magazine*, http://www.slate.com/id/2275733/pagenum/all/.

Heidegger, Martin, *On the Way to Language*, trans. Peter D. Hertz (San Francisco, CA: Harper & Row, 1971).

Heisenbüttel, Helmut, *Über Literatur* (Olten: Walter, 1966).

Hejinan, Lyn, 'The Rejection of Closure,' *The Language of Inquiry* (Berkeley and Los Angeles: University of California Press, 2000) pp.40-58.

Heron, Jerry, Dorothy Hudson, Ross Pudaloff, and Robert Strozier (eds.), *The Ends of Theory* (Detroit, MI: Wayne State University, 1996).

Hocquard, Emmanuel, *Le Voyage à Reykjavik* (Paris: P.O.L., 1997).

Hocquard, Emmanuel, *Dix Leçons de Grammaire: Notes Préparatoires Pour Le Cours de Langage et Ecriture en Troisieme Année: Novembre 2001 – Janvier 2002* (Bordeaux: Ecole des Beaux Arts, 2003).

Hoffmannsthal, Hugo von, *The Whole Difference: Selected Writings of Hugo von Hoffmannsthal*, ed. J.D. McClatchy (Princeton, NJ: Princeton University Press, 2008).

Honig, Edwin, 'A Conversation with Christopher Middleton,' *MLN*, Vol. 91. No.6 (December 1976) pp.1588-1602.

Howe, Susan, *My Emily Dickinson* (New York: New Directions, 2007).

Hulme, Christine, 'Interview with Rosmarie Waldrop,' *12x12: Conversations in 21st Century Poetry and Poetics*, ed. Christina Mengert and Joshua Marie Wilkinson (Iowa City: University of Iowa Press, 2009, pp.76–85).

Hyde, Lewis, *The Gift: Creativity and the Artist in the Modern World* (London: Vintage, 2007).

Jabès, Edmond, *El, or the Last Book*, trans. Rosmarie Waldrop (Middletown, CT: Wesleyan University Press, 1984).

Jabès, Edmond, *The Book of Dialogue*, trans. Rosmarie Waldrop (Middletown, CT: Wesleyan University Press, 1987).

Jabès, Edmond, *From the Book to the Book: An Edmond Jabès Reader*, trans. Rosmarie Waldrop (Hanover and London: Wesleyan University Press, 1991).

Jabès, Edmond, *A Foreigner Carrying in the Crook of his Arm a Tiny Book*, trans. Rosmarie Waldrop (Middletown, CT: Wesleyan University Press, 1993).

Jabès, Edmond, *The Book of Margins*, trans. Rosmarie Waldrop (Chicago and London: The University of Chicago Press, 1993).

Joris, Pierre, *A Nomad Poetics: Essays* (Middletown, CT: Wesleyan University Press, 2003).

Joron, Andrew, *Fathom* (Black Square Editions, 2003).

Joron, Andrew, *The Cry at Zero: Selected Prose* (Denver, CO: Counterpath Press, 2007).

Juvan, Marko, *History and Poetics of Intertextuality*, trans. Timothy Pogačar (West Lafayette, IN: Purdue University Press, 2008).

Kant, Immanuel, *Critique of Pure Reason*, trans. Norman Kemp Smith (Basingstoke and New York: Palgrave, 1929).

Lacoue-Labarthe, Philippe, 'The Caesura of the Speculative,' in Samuel Weber and Henry Sussman (eds.), *Glyph 4* (Baltimore and London: The Johns Hopkins University Press, 1978, pp.57–85).

Lamm, Kimberley, 'Gender in a Minor Key: Rosmarie Waldrop's *A Key into the Language of America*,' How2, Vol.1, No. 8 (Fall, 2002), http://www.asu.edu/pipercwcenter/how2journal/archive/online_archive/v1_8_2002/current/readings/lamm.htm.

Lazer, Hank, 'Meeting in the Book: A Review of *Lavish Absence: Recalling and Rereading Edmond Jabès* by Rosmarie Waldrop,' *Jacket* 23 (August 2003) www.http://jacketmagazine.com/23/lazer-waldr.html.

Lee, Sue-Im, *A Body of Individuals: The Paradox of Community in Contemporary Fiction* (Columbus, OH: The Ohio State University Press, 2009).
Lerner, Ben, 'Apples of Discourse,' *Jacket*, 31 (October 2006), http://jacketmagazine.com/31/lerner-waldrop.html.
Levinas, Emmanuel, *Otherwise than Being or, Beyond Essence*, trans. Alphonso Lingis (Dordrecht: Kluwer Academic Publishers, 1991).
Levinas, Emmanuel, *Proper Names*, trans. Michael B. Smith (Stanford, CA: Stanford University Press, 1996).
Liddell, Henry George and Robert Scott (eds.), *A Greek-English Lexicon* (Oxford: Clarendon, 1925).
Luce, A. and T. Jessop (eds.), *The Works of George Berkeley, Bishop of Cloyne* (London: Thomas Nelson, 1951).
Lurie, Bobbi, 'Meditation on Certainty,' *How2*, Vol. 1. No. 8 (Fall 2002), http://www.asu.edu/pipercwcenter/how2journal/archive/online_archive/v1_8_2002/current/readings/lurie.htm.
MacKendrick, Karmen, *Immemorial Silence* (Albany, NY: State University of New York Press, 2001).
McCaffery, Steve, *North of Intention: Critical Writings, 1973-1986* (Toronto: Nightwood Editions, 1986).
McLennan, Rob, '12 or 20 Questions with Rosmarie Waldrop,' *Rob McLennan's Blog*, 11 January 2008, http://robmclennan.blogspot.co.uk/2008/01/rosmarie-waldrop-was-born-in-kitzingen.html.
McMahon, Fiona, 'Rosmarie Waldrop: A Poetics of Contiguity', *Revue Francaise d'Etudes Americaines*, no. 103 (2005), pp.64-78.
Mach, Ernst, *The Conservation of Energy* (La Salle, IL: Open Court, 1911).
de Man, Paul, *Blindness and Insight: Essays in the Rhetoric of Contemporary Criticism* (London: Methuen, 1983).
Manguel, Alberto, *A History of Reading* (London: HarperCollins, 1996).
Meadows, Deborah, 'Rosmarie Waldrop and the Poetics of Embodied Philosophy,' *How2*, Vol. 1, No. 8 (Fall, 2002), http://www.asu.edu/pipercwcenter/how2journal/archive/online_archive/v1_8_2002/current/readings/meadows.htm.
Mole, Gary D., *Levinas, Blanchot, Jabès: Figures of Estrangement* (Gainesville, FL: University Press of Florida, 1997).
Morrison, Rusty, 'Introducing Small Press Distribution,' http://www.abebooks.com/docs/Community/Featured/spd-omnidawn.shtml.
Mossin, Andrew, 'Networks of the Real in Contemporary Poetry and Poetics: Peter Middleton, Susan Schultz, Rosmarie Waldrop, *Journal of Modern Literature*, Vol. 30, No. 3 (Spring, 2007) pp.143-153.
Moxley, Jennifer, 'A Personal Reminiscence Chronicling the First Documented Case of "The Waldrop Effect,"' *How2*, Vol. 1, No. 8 (Fall 2002), http://www.asu.edu/pipercwcenter/how2journal/archive/online_archive/v1_8_2002/current/readings/moxley.htm.

Munday, Jeremy, *Introducing Translation Studies: Theories and Applications* (London: Routledge, 2001).
Musil, Robert, *The Man Without Qualities, Vol. II, The Like of It Now Happens* (London: Secker & Warburg, 1953).
Nancy, Jean-Luc, *Being Singular Plural*, trans. Robert D. Richardson and Anne E. O'Byrne (Stanford, CA: Stanford University Press, 2000).
Nietzsche, Friedrich, *Thus Spake Zarathustra*, trans. Thomas Common (Ware: Wordsworth Editions, 1997).
Olson, Charles, *Call Me Ishmael* (Baltimore and London: The Johns Hopkins University Press, 1967).
Olson, Charles, *Human Universe and Other Essays*, ed. Donald Allen (New York: Grove, 1967).
Olson, Charles, *Letters of Origin: 1950-1955*, ed. Albert Glover (London: Cape Goliard, 1969).
Olson, Charles, *Selected Writings* (New York: New Directions, 1997).
Osborne, William, 'Marketplace of Ideas: But First, the Bill: A Personal Commentary on American and European Cultural Funding,' *ArtsJournal*, 18th February 2004, http://www.artsjournal.com/artswatch/20040218-11320.shtml.
Ouaknin, Marc-Alain, *The Burnt Book: Reading the Talmud*, trans. Llewellyn Brown (Princeton, NJ: Princeton University Press, 1995).
Palmer, Michael, *Active Boundaries: Selected Essays and Talks* (New York: New Directions, 2008).
Perloff, Marjorie (ed.), *Postmodern Genres* (Norman and London: University of Oaklahoma Press, 1988).
Perloff, Marjorie, 'Towards a Wittgensteinian Poetics,' *Contemporary Literature*, Vol. 33, No. 2, Special Issue: American Poetry of the 1980s (Summer 1992) pp.191-213.
Perloff, Marjorie, 'Collage and Poetry,' *Encyclopedia of Aesthetics*, ed. Michael Kelly (New York: Oxford University Press, 1998) pp.384-387.
Perloff, Marjorie, *Frank O'Hara: Poet Among Painters* (Chicago and London: The University of Chicago Press, 1998).
Perloff, Marjorie, 'A Small Periplus Along an Edge: Rosmarie Waldrop's AutoGraphs,' *How2*, Vol.1, No.8 (Fall, 2002), http://www.asu.edu/pipercwcenter/how2journal/archive/online_archive/v1_8_2002/current/readings/perloff.htm.
Pike, Burton, *Robert Musil: An Introduction to His Work* (Port Washington, N.Y., and London: Kennikat Press, 1972).
Pound, Ezra, *Literary Essays of Ezra Pound* (New York: New Directions, 1935).
Pound, Ezra, *Selected Prose, 1909-1965*, ed. William Cookson (New York: New Directions, 1975).
Pound, Ezra, *Pound's Cavalcanti*, ed. David Anderson (Princeton, NJ: Princeton University Press, 1983).

Ravnikar, Nicholas Michael, 'Pre-Calculus for Small Press Publishers', *Woodland Pattern*, http://woodlandpattern.blogspot.com/2010/03/pre-calculus-for-small-press-publishers.html.

Reed, Brian, '"Splice of Life": Rosmarie Waldrop Renews Collage,' *How2*, Vol. 1, No. 8 (Fall, 2002), http://www.asu.edu/pipercwcenter/how2journal/archive/online_archive/v1_8_2002/current/readings/reed.htm.

Retallack, Joan, 'A Conversation with Rosmarie Waldrop,' *Contemporary Literature*, Vol. 40, No. 3 (Autumn, 1999) pp.329-377.

Retallack, Joan, 'A Conversation Between Joan Retallack and Rosmarie Waldrop, Pt.2,' How2, Vol. 1, No. 8 (Fall, 2002), http://www.asu.edu/pipercwcenter/how2journal/archive/online_archive/v1_8_2002/current/readings/retallack.htm.

Rimmon-Kenan, Shlomith, *Narrative Fiction* (London: Methuen, 1983).

Robinson, Douglas, *Western Translation Theory: From Herodotus to Nietzsche* (Manchester: St Jerome Publishing, 1997).

Royet-Journoud, Claude, *Le Renversement* (Paris: Gallimard, 1972).

Schmidt, Michael, *Lives of the Poets* (New York: Knopf, 1999).

Schmidt, Michael, 'A Little Carcanet Anthology,' *The North*, No.48 (2011), pp.42–45.

Scholem, Gershom, *On the Kabbalah and Its Symbolism*, trans. Ralph Manheim (New York: Schocken, 1969).

Scott, Grant F., *Selected Letters of John Keats* (Cambridge, MA: Harvard University Press, 2005).

Silliman, Ron, *The New Sentence* (New York: Roof Books, 1989).

Smith Nash, Susan, 'Two Score and More', *Review of Contemporary Fiction* (Summer 2003).

Stein, Gertrude, *Lectures in America* (New York: Random House, 1935).

Stein, Gertrude, *Writings and Lectures: 1909-1945*, ed. Patricia Meyerowitz (New York: Penguin, 1971).

Stein, Gertrude, *How Writing is Written* (Los Angeles: Black Sparrow, 1974).

Stein, Gertrude, *The Previously Uncollected Writings of Gertrude Stein, Vol. II*, ed. Robert Haas (Los Angeles: Black Sparrow Press, 1974).

Stein, Gertrude, *A Stein Reader*, ed. Ulla E. Dydo (Evanston, IL: Northwestern University Press, 1993).

Stein, Gertrude, *Tender Buttons* (Mineola, NY: Dover Publications, 1998).

Steiner, George, *After Babel: Aspects of Language and Translation* (London: Oxford University Press, 1975).

Storhaug, Glenn, 'On Printing Aloud', http://www.fiveseasonspress.com/printingaloud.pdf.

Swales, Martin, 'Theoretical Reflections on the Work of W.G. Sebald,' *W.G. Sebald: A Critical Companion*, ed. J.J. Long and Anne Whitehead (Edinburgh: Edinburgh University Press, 2004).

Taylor, John, 'Two Cultures of the Prose Poem,' *Michigan Quarterly Review*, Vol. XLIV, No. 2, (Spring 2005), http://hdl.handle.net/2027/spo.act2080.0044.223.

Venuti, Lawrence (ed.), *Rethinking Translation: Discourse, Subjectivity, Ideology* (London: Routledge, 1992).
Venuti, Lawrence (ed.), *The Translation Studies Reader* (London: Routledge, 2004).
Waldrop, Keith, *The Garden of Effort* (Providence, RI: Burning Deck, 1975).
Waldrop, Rosmarie and Keith (eds.), *A Century in Two Decades: A Burning Deck Anthology, 1961-1981* (Providence, RI: Burning Deck, 1982).
Waldrop, Rosmarie, *Against Language? 'dissatisfaction with language' as theme and as impulse towards experiments in twentieth century poetry* (The Hague: Mouton, 1971).
Waldrop, Rosmarie, *The Aggressive Ways of the Casual Stranger* (New York: Random House, 1972).
Waldrop, Rosmarie, 'Nothing Has Changed,' *Living Hand*, 4 (Winter 1975), pp.74-94.
Waldrop, Rosmarie, *The Road is Everywhere or, Stop This Body* (Columbia, MI: Open Places, 1978).
Waldrop, Rosmarie, *Peculiar Motions* (Berkeley, CA: Kelsey St. Press, 1990).
Waldrop, Rosmarie, *Lawn of Excluded Middle* (Providence, RI: Tender Buttons, 1993).
Waldrop, Rosmarie, *A Key into the Language of America* (New York: New Directions, 1994).
Waldrop, Rosmarie, *Split Infinites* (Philadelphia, PA: Singing Horse Press, 1998).
Waldrop, Rosmarie, *The Hanky of Pippin's Daughter* (Evanston, IL: Northwestern University Press, 2000).
Waldrop, Rosmarie, *A Form/of Taking/It All* (Evanston, IL: Northwestern University Press, 2001).
Waldrop, Rosmarie, *Ceci n'est pas Keith, Ceci n'est pas Rosmarie* (Providence, RI: Burning Deck, 2002).
Waldrop, Rosmarie, *Lavish Absence: Recalling and Rereading Edmond Jabès* (Middletown, CT: Wesleyan University Press, 2002).
Waldrop, Rosmarie, *Blindsight* (New York: New Directions, 2003).
Waldrop, Rosmarie, *Love, Like Pronouns* (Richmond, CA: Omnidawn, 2003).
Waldrop, Rosmarie, *Dissonance (if you are interested)* (Tuscaloosa, AL: The University of Alabama Press, 2005).
Waldrop, Rosmarie, 'Velocity but no location,' *Salt Magazine*, Issue 2 (April 2008), n.p.
Waldrop, Rosmarie, *Driven to Abstraction* (New York: New Directions, 2010).
Waldrop, Rosmarie, 'Response,' *Double Room: A Journal of Prose Poetry and Flash Fiction*, http://doubleroomjournal.com/issue_one/RW_ResBio.html.
Whitehead, Alfred North, *Modes of Thought* (New York: Macmillan, 1938).
Williams, Roger, *A Key into the Language of America* (Bedford, MA: Applewood Books, 1997).

Williams, Roger, *The Complete Writings of Roger Williams, Vol. 1*, ed. Edwin Gaustad (New York, Russell and Russell, 2007).
Williams, William Carlos, *Patterson* (New York: New Directions, 1963).
Wittgenstein, Ludwig, *Tractatus Logico-Philosophicus*, trans. D.F. Pears and B.F. McGuinness (London: Routledge, 1961).
Wittgenstein, Ludwig, *Last Writings on the Philosophy of Psychology: The Inner and the Outer*, vol.2 (Oxford: Blackwell, 1992).
Wittgenstein, Ludwig, *Philosophical Investigations* (Oxford: Blackwell, 2009).
Wolin, Richard (ed.), *The Heidegger Controversy: A Critical Reader* (Cambridge, MA: MIT Press, 1993).
Woods, Tim, *The Poetics of the Limit: Ethics and Politics in Modern and Contemporary American Poetry* (Basingstoke: Palgrave, 2002).

Acknowledgements

This book has been in the planning for some time, and various individuals have played a part, direct or otherwise. I would like to thank them all, but particularly: Sarah Barnsley, Andrew Biswell, Conor Carville, Josh Cohen, Robert Eaglestone, Robert Hampson, Tony Frazer, Lars Iyer, Rupert Loydell, Adam Rounce, David Rudrum, Berthold Schoene, Ian Seed, Scott Thurston, and all the students in the Department of English at Manchester Metropolitan University who have taken my 'American Poetics' module over the years.

I would like to extend very grateful thanks to Rosmarie Waldrop, for her constant generosity, kindness, and support throughout the course of this project. I would particularly like to thank her for always taking the time to respond in detail to my questions, and for the various surprise, and very gladly received, packages of books which have sporadically come through the post since we first met at a conference in Bochum, Germany, in 2005.

I would also like to thank my wife, Emily, and our son, Elijah, to whom this book is dedicated, for their constant love, patience, and encouragement, and without whom this book would not have been written. *Our inclusive views are mosaics.*

* * *

Some sections of the book have appeared previously in slightly different versions elsewhere:

'The Poetics of Emergency,' *Jacket*, 32 (2007).

'Without Location: Rosmarie Waldrop and the Poetics of the Neuter' in Kornelia Freitag (ed.), *Another Language: Poetic Experiments in Britain and North America* (Münster, Lit-Verlag, 2008), pp.251-262.

'Rosmarie Waldrop and Theories of Translation,' *452F: Journal of Theory of Literature and Comparative Literature*, No. 7 (July 2012), pp.24-39.

'Reading Rosmarie Waldrop', *New Walk*, 6 (April 2013), pp.18-24.

The Author

Nikolai Duffy is a Senior Lecturer in American Literature at Manchester Metropolitan University, and the founding editor of Like This Press. He has published various essays on experimental writing practices, contemporary poetics, and small press publishing. Recent poetry has appeared in *Shearsman*, *Stride*, *Blackbox Manifold* and *E.ratio*; his book, *The Little Shed of Various Lamps*, was published by Very Small Kitchen in 2013.